S0-EJP-136

SSIA

DNJEPR

BUG

PRUTH

CUMANS OR POLO

SEA OF AZOV

CRIMEA

EGS

Varna

BLACK SEA

opolis

Adrianople

Constantinople

RACE

Nicomedia

Nicaea

SULTANATE OF ICONIUM

Myriocephalon

Iconium

Smyrna

Miletus

RHODES

Seleucia

Antioch

CYPRUS

Tripolis

THE BYZANTINE EMPIRE
at the time of Manuel's death, 1180

Tyre

Acre

Jerusalem

BYZANTIUM
and the
DANUBE
FRONTIER

BYZANTIUM
and the
DANUBE
FRONTIER

*A study of the relations between Byzantium, Hungary,
and the Balkans during the period of the Comneni*

By
Andrew B. Urbansky

TWAYNE PUBLISHERS, INC.
31 Union Square West   : :   New York, N. Y. 10003

Preface

THE period of the Comneni, a last revival of Byzantine grandeur and brilliance, is well known to the scholar of Byzantine history. The First and Second Crusades, the rising power of the Normans in Sicily, the efforts of Frederick Barbarossa to win control of Italy and his conflict with Pope Alexander III form the background to this period, during which the contacts between Byzantium and western Europe were more intimate and the frictions more frequent than in any previous period of Byzantine history. This resulted in large measure from the ambitious schemes of the Emperor Manuel Comnenus, who endeavored to secure for himself the imperial crown of Rome and to restore the unity of Christian Europe under the leadership of Byzantium.

The greater interest which is understandably concentrated on the western policies of the Comnenian emperors is apt to obscure the role and significance of the northern neighbors of Byzantium in the Balkans and the Danube basin. This is particularly true of Hungary, which during the Comnenian period established not only political and commercial relations but also dynastic ties with the Byzantine Empire. The role, however, which Hungary played in the foreign policies of Manuel, has been treated rather superficially by modern historians.

Because of her geographical situation, Hungary sometimes formed a barrier and sometimes a bridge between the Byzantine Empire and the West, and consequently represented an obstacle, or occasionally a valuable asset, in the schemes of Byzantine diplomacy. Closer dynastic ties had been established between Byzantium and Hungary through the marriage of the Emperor John II Comnenus to a Hungarian princess. With the accession of Manuel Comnenus, who on his mother's side was grandson of King Ladislas of Hungary, Byzantine policies towards Hungary assumed a more definite pattern.

Manuel's plans for the restoration of his influence in the West first brought him into conflict with the new rising power of the Norman-Sicilian kingdom. Later, after the accession of Frederick Barbarossa, a rivalry developed between Byzantium and the German Empire. Although Manuel's main objective necessarily remained the control of Italy, the strategic and political importance of the Balkans and of Hungary revealed itself when a revolt of his Serbian vassals forced Manuel to delay a major military action in southern Italy. The Serbians were supported by Hungary, which had conflicting interests with Byzantium on the Adriatic coast of Dalmatia. While the Serbians eventually were forced into submission, the problem of securing control of the Balkans and defending the Danube frontier, as well as that of preventing Hungary from falling into the German orbit, involved the Byzantine Empire in a long series of military and diplomatic moves against Hungary.

The aim of the present study is to throw light on the development of Byzantine-Hungarian relations during the Comnenian period, and in particular to demonstrate the impact of the Hungarian problem on Manuel's western political schemes. This problem first caused an irreparable delay of a major military action against southern Italy. Subsequently the conflict with Hungary tied down the military and diplomatic forces of the empire for more than two decades. When Manuel finally succeeded in securing control of Hungary through a diplomatic marriage, he had to face an entirely new and unfavorable power situation in Italy and also in the East. Thus, the protracted involvement in Hungarian affairs was largely responsible for the failure of Manuel's ambitious western designs. It was an empire already exhausted militarily and financially which received the final blow in the disastrous defeat at Myriocephalon.

In the preparation of the present study I am deeply indebted to Dr. Marshall W. Baldwin, Professor of History at New York University, who was of the greatest assistance in suggesting new sources and offering precious guidance throughout the entire work.

I also wish to express my deep appreciation for the generous grant given to me by the University of Bridgeport, which greatly aided the publication of this book.

Proper names in the text with well known English form are spelled according to the English spelling; other names generally follow the normal national (German, Hungarian, etc.) spelling.

A. U.

Bridgeport, Conn.
September 1967

Contents

	Preface	5
1.	Introduction	11
2.	Hungarian Expansion Southward	32
3.	Manuel's Western Policy and the Balkans	51
4.	Struggle for the Control of Hungary	67
5.	Hungary in the Byzantine Orbit	89
6.	Western Policies and Hungarian Relations During the Last Decades of Manuel's Reign	112
7.	Conclusion	125
	Notes and References	131
	Bibliography	147
	Genealogical Table	162
	Index	165

CHAPTER I

Introduction

THE earliest contacts between Byzantium and the Hungarians date back to the last decade of the ninth century, when the Magyars or Hungarians appeared for the first time on the eastern European scene. In the late ninth century the Magyars (Hungarians, Onogurs, Ugrians, or, as the Islamic and Greek sources frequently call them, Turks) were driven from their settlements along the northern shores of the Black Sea by the Pechenegs, or Patzinaks, another nomadic people probably of Turkish origin. After this attack, around 889, the Magyars, then in loose tribal organization, entered the lowlands bounded by the southeastern Carpathians and the Danube and Dniester rivers. It was during their relatively short stay in this region that they came into contact with the Byzantine world.[1]

The appearance of the Hungarians found Europe in one of the most crucial periods of its history. Simultaneously with the disintegration of the Carolingian empire, the West was threatened by new waves of invaders, the Normans from the north, the Saracens from the south, and these were soon joined by the Magyars in the east. At the same time, the Byzantine Empire was gradually emerging from a period marked by serious losses.

The iconoclast controversy, which had disturbed the life of the Byzantine state since the Emperor Leo III issued

his first edict against images in 726, had important consequences in the international political field as well. First of
all, it widened the gap between Byzantium and the West,
weakening the concept of a universal Christian empire, and
thus paved the way for the rise of a new empire in the
West, the Frankish empire of the Carolingians. The iconoclast period also saw the collapse of important Byzantine
power positions in the West, notably Ravenna, lost to the
Lombards (751) and later to the papal state; Sicily, lost
to the Saracens (827-843) ; and Venice, a former Byzantine
possession which gradually rose to independent status during the first half of the ninth century and became the
only Adriatic power capable of containing the assaults of
the Saracen and Narentan-Slavonic pirates against the Dalmatian coastal cities.

It was only in the East and the Balkans that the Byzantine Empire could hold its own. Internal dissensions within
the caliphate of Bagdad, following Harun al Rashid's death,
relieved the Arab pressure on the eastern frontiers. And
in the Balkans the Emperor Leo V succeeded in concluding
a thirty year truce with the Bulgarians in 815.[2]

This period of decline of Byzantine political influence
and military power was brought to a close with the sup-
pression of iconoclasm during the reign of Theophilus' son,
Michael III (842-867). The resumption of a more aggressive foreign policy was marked by a successful attack
against Egypt in 853 and by the great Byzantine victory
over the Arabs in Asia Minor in 863.

The recovery continued under Basil I (867-886), founder
of the Macedonian dynasty. The resurgence of Byzantine power under the Macedonian emperors coincides with
the appearance of the Hungarians in Europe. During this
period the empire regained its foothold in southern Italy
from the Saracens, checked the Moslem advance in Asia
Minor, and brought the Slavs and Bulgarians of the Balkan

Peninsula under lasting Byzantine cultural and political influence.

In order to check the Arab menace in southern Italy, Basil entered into alliance with the Emperor Louis II, son of Lothair, who had inherited the imperial title and Italy as part of the Carolingian heritage. With the aid of a Byzantine fleet, Louis reconquered Bari in 871 from the Saracens, and after Louis' death in 875 the city passed under the protection of the Byzantine governor of Otranto. In the last years of Basil's reign Byzantine authority had been restored not only in the extreme southern part of the peninsula, in Apulia and Calabria, but it had been extended over some local rulers of southern Italy, like the prince of Salerno, the duke of Benevento, and the bishop of Naples, all of whom became vassals of the Byzantine emperor.[3]

Basil also reaffirmed Byzantine authority over the eastern coast of the Adriatic, where Saracen pirates had laid siege to the city of Ragusa. In 868 he sent a fleet to the aid of the beleaguered city and the Saracens were forced to abandon the siege. The creation of the Byzantine province or *theme* of Dalmatia probably closely followed the expedition which relieved Ragusa from the Saracens. The new province included the islands and coastal area of the northeastern Adriatic with the cities of Zara (Zadar, or Jadra), Spalato (Asphalathos, or Split), Traù (Trogir), and Ragusa (Dubrovnik).[4]

Basil even attempted to reassert virtual Byzantine supremacy over Venice by conferring the title of a high-ranking imperial office, that of a *protospatharius*, on the Doge Ursus Particiacus.[5] By the middle of the ninth century, however, the independence of the republic of Venice was more or less a recognized fact. The city, which at the beginning of the ninth century still formed an integral part of the Byzantine Empire, had been occupied by the Franks in 809-

810. Negotiations between Charlemagne and the Emperor Nicephorus, and later his successor, Michael I, led to the treaty of Aix-la-Chapelle in 812 by which Byzantium recognized the imperial title of the Frankish emperor, who in turn recognized Venice and the Dalmatian cities as Byzantine possessions.

The government in Constantinople, however, was unable to provide adequate defense against the attacks of Saracen and Slavonic pirates. During the first half of the ninth century Venice began to act independently, as the only power on the northern Adriatic which, left on her own, was strong enough to resist such attacks and also to give support to the Dalmatian cities. In 840 Venice signed a treaty of alliance with the Frankish Emperor Lothair I, who guaranteed the Venetian possessions. This treaty can perhaps be regarded as the first independent diplomatic move of the republic of St. Mark.[6] The independence of Venice was no longer challenged by the government in Constantinople, even after Basil I, in the second half of the ninth century, restored Byzantine sovereignty over the eastern coast of the Adriatic.

The important role which Venice played in the defense of the Dalmatian cities, and the common interests of the empire and the republic in the face of the Saracen and Adriatic Slav aggressions, probably accounted for the Byzantine government's failure to stress Venetian recognition of Byzantine supremacy. Basil I, as mentioned above, was content to bestow a high imperial office upon the doge, but in his further dealings with the republic he treated Venice as an independent state. This policy was also followed by subsequent emperors.[7]

During the reign of Basil II (976-1025), which marked the apogee of Byzantine ascendancy, Venice rose to the position of first class maritime power on the Adriatic. Heavily engaged in a struggle with the Bulgars for control of the Balkans, Basil II concluded an alliance with the republic and in 992 granted preferential treatment to Venetian trade within the empire, under the condition that Byzantium could use Venetian ships for troop-transportations to Italy.[8] From 998 on, in fact, the doge of Venice was the representative of Byzantine authority in the theme of Dalmatia, for Basil II accorded the title of *Dux Dalmatiae* to the Doge Peter Orseolo and charged him, as *proconsul* and *patricius* of the empire, with the defense of the province against the Arabs and the Slav pirates.[9]

Peter Orseolo, whose grandson was to become king of Hungary, made his triumphal entry into the Dalmatian cities as representative of the Byzantine emperor in 1001. This event served as basis for future Venetian claims of control over Dalmatia, and also marked the birth of a new power on the Adriatic.[10]

The last quarter of the ninth century also witnessed the emergence of Germany as predominant power in Central Europe. In 887 the German princes elected Arnulf, the illegitimate grandson of Louis the German, to the throne of the eastern Frankish kingdom. Arnulf restored the royal authority, checked the raids of the Danes and Slavs, and with the aid of the Hungarian newcomers, reduced the power of the Moravian kingdom established by Svatopluk in the second half of the ninth century on the eastern borders of Germany, in the valley of the Danube.

But the resurgence of central authority under Arnulf proved to be ephemeral. His weak successors, Louis the Child and Conrad of Franconia, were unable to control the German dukes or to defend the country against Hungarian raids. It was only after the election of Henry the Fowler, under the rulers of the Saxon dynasty, that the German kingdom appeared in the mid-tenth century as a strong new rival to the Byzantine Empire. While Henry was primarily interested in consolidating his authority over Germany, his son and successor, Otto the Great, dreamed of the restoration of Charlemagne's empire. In his first Italian expedition (951), Otto rescued Adelaide, the widow of Lothair, king of Italy, from the usurper Berengar of Ivrea. Through his marriage with Adelaide he secured control of the kingdom of Italy. Ten years later, when Pope John XII appealed to him for help against Berengar, Otto marched south again, entered Rome, and in February, 962 was crowned Roman emperor by the pope.

The assumption of the imperial title was an open challenge to Byzantine power in Italy. Otto extended his control south from Rome over Capua and Benevento, and after unsuccessful negotiations between his envoy, Liudprand, bishop of Cremona, and the Emperor Nicephorus Phocas, Otto invaded the Byzantine theme of Apulia, but was defeated in an attempt to capture Bari. German-Byzantine relations improved only after the accession of John Tzimisces to the Byzantine throne. New negotiations started, leading to the marriage alliance between Otto's son, the future Emperor Otto II, and the Byzantine princess, Theophano. At the same time, a treaty confirmed Otto I in the possession of Capua and Benevento, but he had to give up all attempts against Apulia. Thus by the second half of the tenth century Italy became the primary object of a rivalry between Byzantium and the medieval German empire. Another area which was to be a source of contention between the two empires during the next two centuries was the mid-Danube basin, site of the first permanent home of the Hungarian people in Europe.

The events which led to the permanent settlement of the Hungarians in the Danube basin towards the end of the nir.h century are particularly associated with the relations between the Byzantine Empire and the Bulgarians. During the reign of the Emperor Leo VI (896-912) there occurred a dispute over certain grievances of Bulgarian merchants in Thessalonica. When his protests were disregarded by the Byzantine government, Simeon, the Bulgarian tsar, who also entertained certain ambitious schemes for Bulgarian hegemony over the Balkans, invaded Byzantine territory in Macedonia and Thrace, and in 894 his armies threatened Constantinople itself. Since the major part of the imperial forces was engaged in a campaign against the Arabs, in 895 Leo VI invited the nomadic Magyars, or Hungarians, to enter into alliance with the empire and invade Bulgarian territory.[11]

It will be recalled that the Hungarians were then situated in the lowlands between the Carpathians and the lower Danube. They accepted the offer and, after crossing the Danube in Byzantine ships, attacked and defeated the Bulgarians in several battles. Simeon now won over to his side the Pechenegs, who were eastern neighbors of the Hungarians. With their aid, he inflicted a severe defeat on the Magyars, who eventually abandoned their settlements on the lower Danube and, in their retreat before the Pechenegs, crossed the eastern Carpathians at several points. Probably in 896 they entered the great plains of the middle Danube, the site of their future permanent home.[12] This territory was not entirely unknown to the Hungarians, for as has already been mentioned, Hungarian auxiliaries participated, only a few years earlier in 892, in Arnulf's campaign against the Moravian kingdom of Svatopluk.[13]

Thus the Hungarians, at the time of their first appearance on the European scene, came almost simultaneously into close contact, through military alliances, with the two

major powers of Europe, the Byzantine Empire in the East
and the German "Roman" Empire in the West.[14] Although
the conversion of the Hungarians to Latin Christianity a
century later strengthened the ties which connected them
with the West, the two-faced character of the new Hungarian state was to determine its foreign policy under the
Arpád dynasty for the next two hundred years. During
this period they had to balance East against West, entering
alternatively into alliances with one against the other and
opposing the persistent influence of both.

According to Hungarian tradition the seven Hungarian
tribes elected their first common leader during their stay
in the lower Danube area. This leader was Almos, tribal
chieftain of the Megyer or Magyar tribe. His son Arpád
assumed the leadership shortly before the Hungarians entered the middle Danube basin in 895 or 896 through the
mountain passes of the northeastern Carpathians.[15.]

For a century following the conquest of their new land
the Hungarians remained pagans and maintained a pre-
dominantly tribal organization. Marauding expeditions were
conducted against western Europe, Germany, Italy, and
France, and occasionally against the Byzantine Empire. It
was only after the disastrous defeat of one of their armies
by the German king (later emperor) Otto the Great, at
Lechfeld in 955, that the Hungarians, under the leadership
of Arpád's great-grandson, Géza, finally gave up their
nomadic and barbarian way of life and began to build up
a more centralized and stable political organization in the
central Danube valley.

Despite the early contacts with the Byzantine Empire,
the new Hungarian state began from the first to look west-
ward. This western orientation was early marked by the
conversion of Géza and his son Stephen to Latin Christianity. There followed the marriage of Stephen to a
Bavarian princess, Gisella, and Stephen's receiving a royal

crown from Pope Sylvester II. With this he was crowned in 1000 as the first king of Hungary.

Stephen's western policy and his work of consolidating the monarchy were jeopardized by the loss of his only son, Emeric. After Emeric's untimely death in his early twenties, Stephen designated his nephew, Peter, as heir-presumptive to the throne. Peter was the son of Stephen's sister and Otto Orseolo, doge of Venice. He was regarded with mistrust, as a foreigner who leaned mainly on the support of Germans and Italians. Thus when Peter, in order to secure the support of the German Empire, recognized the suzerainty of the Emperor Henry III, a national and pagan uprising deposed him in 1046. The rebels invited to the throne another member of the Arpád dynasty, Andrew, whose father, a cousin of Stephen I, remained pagan, and whose family had, as a consequence, been exiled to Russia. In exile Andrew embraced Christianity and married Anastasia, daughter of Yaroslav the Wise, prince of Kiev.[16]

With Andrew's accession to the throne the German influence in Hungary was brought at least temporarily to an end. When Henry III attempted to assert his overlordship over Hungary, Andrew repudiated the ties of vassalage and with the aid of his younger brother, Prince Béla, a talented military leader, successfully fought off several armed German interventions. Peace between Hungary and the German Empire was restored only through the mediation of Pope Leo IX after Henry III's death in 1056, and it was sealed in 1058 by the engagement of Andrew's son Salomon to Henry's daughter Judith.

Meanwhile, the attention of Hungarian foreign policy in the second half of the eleventh century was also turning toward Byzantium. In the tenth century marauding expeditions of Hungarian troops repeatedly ravaged Byzantine territory, and in 958 they were defeated by imperial troops in Thrace. Nevertheless, the flexible Byzantine diplomacy succeeded in establishing occasional friendly contacts with the Hungarians. Hungarian embassies frequently visited the court of Constantine Porphyrogenitus. In 943 a treaty was concluded and commercial relations were established between Hungary and Byzantium. Several prominent Hungarian leaders, during their stay at the Byzantine court, embraced Christianity and received the dignity of Roman *patrician*, yet attempts to bring a larger number of Hungarians into the Byzantine Church failed.[17]

Under Géza and his son Stephen, Hungary's political, cultural, and religious orientation became increasingly western, but relations with the Byzantine Empire during the first half of the eleventh century remained excellent.[18] During the reign of the first Hungarian king, Stephen I, four Byzantine monasteries were established in Hungary and placed under royal protection. In the campaign of the Emperor Basil II against the Bulgarian Tsar Samuel, Hungarian auxiliaries aided the Byzantine troops at the occupation of Ochrida in 1016.[19]

These friendly relations deteriorated rather rapidly under Andrew I and his successors, who attempted to profit by the serious internal and external difficulties which beset the Byzantine Empire after the end of the Macedonian dynasty. The last male member of this dynasty, Constantine VIII, died in 1028, and from then until 1056 ineffective rulers shared the imperial power with his daughters, Zoe and then Theodora, who preserved the principle of legitimacy in the succession by representing the Macedonian dynasty on the throne. In 1055, Theodora, Constantine VIII's last surviving daughter, ascended the throne alone. The period which followed her brief reign brought not only a bitter struggle for power between the civil administrators of the imperial palace and the commanders of the army, but also painful military and territorial losses in the peripheral areas of the empire. Between Theodora's death in 1056

and the final accession of the Comnenian dynasty with
Alexius I in 1081, the Byzantine possessions in southern
Italy were gradually lost to the Normans, and in the same
period Asia Minor and Syria were laid open to the Seljuk
Turk invaders by the disastrous battle of Manzikert in
1071.[20]

It was during this period of relative weakness that Hungarian attacks against Byzantine territory were resumed.
The first campaign was conducted by Andrew I between
1057 and 1059. The Hungarians fought off an invasion of
Pechenegs who had invaded Hungary after passing through
Byzantine territory. Hungarian troops then followed the
invaders into Byzantine territory and occupied the region
of Sirmium. Although their further advance was checked
by the Emperor Isaac Comnenus, the peace treaty he concluded with Andrew I at Sophia apparently left Sirmium
in Hungarian possession.[21]

In the last year of Andrew's reign an open hostility
broke out between the king and his brother, Prince Béla,
the brilliant and popular military leader. Béla had been
recognized by Andrew as heir to the throne, but when a son,
Salomon, was born to Andrew, he changed the right of
succession in his favor, and Béla was forced to recognize
Salomon's priority. When Andrew I died in 1060, Béla
secured the throne for himself by military force and, with
the support of the majority of the nation, turned against
the eight-year-old Salomon, who fled to the protection of
the Emperor Henry IV, his future brother-in-law.

Béla I's short reign (1060-1063) left excellent memories
in Hungarian history. He restored internal order and kept
his country at peace with both East and West. Béla's sons
did not oppose Salomon's claims after their father's death,
and he was able to return from the court of Henry IV to
become king.

With Salomon's return a new Hungarian campaign was

opened against Byzantine territory. The pretext was again provided by the Pechenegs. Around the middle of the eleventh century these warlike nomads crossed the lower Danube and sought refuge in Byzantine territory from the attacks of other nomadic peoples, the Cumans and the Oguz. The Byzantine government eventually allowed them to settle within the borders of the empire and used them as a garrison along the northern frontier. The undisciplined bands of Pechenegs, however, frequently directed their attacks across the Danube into southern Hungary.

Following such a Pecheneg inroad, Salomon's army laid siege to the important Byzantine outpost of Belgrade, which surrendered after three months to the Hungarians (1064).[22] Apparently the empire, which at the same time was under heavy attack by the Normans, as well as by the Seljuk Turks and their nomadic kinfolk, the Oguz, was not in a position to meet the Hungarian invasion into the Balkans with sufficient forces. The campaign dragged on and, according to the Byzantine and Hungarian sources, the Hungarian army penetrated as far as Naissus (Niš).[23]

The Byzantine Empire had ample reason to watch with concern the southward expansion of the Hungarian kingdom. No longer was it a loosely organized nomadic force, but a strong, well organized Christian state which, moreover, had established and maintained good relations with its powerful western neighbor, the German Empire. The political and military situation of the Byzantine Empire became especially critical in the year 1071 with the battle of Manzikert, and the loss of Bari, the last Byzantine stronghold in Italy, to the Normans. Already the celebrated Norman leader, Robert Guiscard, was preparing a direct attack against the empire in the Balkans and perhaps aspired to place the crown of Byzantium on his own head.

No doubt these circumstances prompted the Emperor Michael VII Ducas to enter into peace negotiations with the Hungarians. However, he sent his emissaries not to King Salomon, but to his eldest cousin, Prince Géza. Whether the bypassing of the king was intentional is not clear. It is true that Géza's wife, Synnadena, was Greek, the daughter of Theodulos Synnadenus and niece of the Byzantine general and future emperor, Nicephorus Botaniates. At any rate, it proved to be a clever diplomatic move, because it brought into the open an already existing mutual distrust and jealousy between the king and his cousins, Princes Géza and Ladislas. While Salomon naturally felt his royal authority challenged, Géza responded to the attention of the Byzantine court by releasing all Greek prisoners who were under his power.[24]

It came indeed as a fortunate turn for the empire, when the enmity between the king and the princes led to an armed conflict in 1074. The king relied on the help of his brother-in-law, the German Emperor Henry IV, while the princes were aided by Otto, duke of Moravia. In the ensuing battle of Mogyoród near Buda-Pest, Salomon's forces were routed, but the king himself escaped from the battle and established himself in the western stronghold of Pozsony (Pressburg) near the German-Hungarian border.[25]

The consequences of these developments marked the beginning of a new phase in Byzantine-Hungarian relations. Prince Géza, possibly even before the final showdown with Salomon, was anxious to secure papal blessing for his actions and turned for support and advice to the Holy See.

Since the middle of the eleventh century important changes had occurred in the position of the papacy. Although the schism of 1054 between the Eastern and Western Churches did not then seem irreparable, it did nonetheless confirm the independence of the Byzantine Church from Rome. At the same time the papacy became increasingly independent from the influence of secular power, especially when the death of the German Emperor Henry III in 1056, as well as the long minority of his successor, Henry IV, freed the pope from the tutelage of the western emperor. The independent position of the papacy was expressed in two important acts of Pope Nicholas II. One was his treaty signed at Melfi, in 1059 with Robert Guiscard, who was recognized as duke of Calabria, Apulia, and the Lombard principalities under the suzerainty of the Holy See in return for Norman military aid. The other was Nicholas' decree of 1059 which excluded all secular influence from papal elections and placed them solely in the hands of the College of Cardinals.

The independence of the Church from all lay authority was one of the leading ideas of the pontificate of the energetic Gregory VII (1073-1085).[26] Under his leadership the reformed papacy became increasingly active in diplomatic developments.

When Prince Géza asked for papal support, Gregory accepted the role of arbiter in the dispute which had developed between the Hungarian king and the Árpád princes and seemed to approve the claims of Géza, who accused his cousin the king of breaches of faith and peace. It was presumably of significance also that King Salomon was allied with the Emperor Henry IV, the pope's opponent in the famous controversy over lay investiture. At any rate, Pope Gregory VII assured Géza of his apostolic protection, while Salomon sought diplomatic support and military aid at the court of Henry IV. When the forces sent by the emperor turned out to be inadequate, Salomon also made, somewhat belatedly, an appeal to the pope, asking him to do justice in the dispute with the princes. He was, however, reprimanded by Gregory VII, who reminded him that the Hungarian crown was a possession of the Church of Rome and that Salomon had committed a grave error in accepting it as fief from the German emperor.[27]

When Salomon failed to give up the friendship of Henry

IV, the pope was prepared to throw his full support behind Géza. There was, however, one condition: that Géza acknowledge papal overlordship over Hungary, i.e., that he accept the crown of Hungary as a papal fief and renounce the right of lay investiture. Thus the crown of Hungary seemed to become another object of rivalry between Henry IV, who maintained that Hungary since the time of Henry III had been an imperial fief, and the pope, who vindicated apostolic supremacy over Hungary, basing his claim upon the fact that Stephen, the first Hungarian king, had received the symbol of the monarchy from Pope Sylvester II.

It is easy to understand why in this situation Prince Géza apparently decided to free himself from both imperial and papal claims and to turn to the Byzantine Empire, asking the Emperor Michael VII Ducas to recognize him as king of Hungary and to send him a royal crown as symbol of recognition. From the fact that Géza requested a crown from the Byzantine emperor, we can conclude only that the crown of St. Stephen was probably in the possession of Salomon, for certainly it was not Géza's intention to place himself under Byzantine overlordship.[28] In view of the rather weak diplomatic and military position of the Byzantine Empire in the second half of the eleventh century, the recognition by the Byzantine emperor and the acceptance of a crown from him apparently gave Prince Géza no cause for concern. Rather, the action reflects what was gradually becoming the customary policy of the Árpáds, to balance East versus West and to seek the support of one against the other.

Emperor Michael VII Ducas, who had already given signs of a friendly attitude towards Géza during the Serbian campaign, granted his recognition and sent him a crown which bears in enamel the portraits of the Emperors Constantine Porphyrogenitus and Michael Ducas, as well as one of Géza. Under the picture of Géza the Greek inscrip-

tion reads: "King of Turcia." This crown was later attached
to the original crown given to Stephen I by Pope Sylvester
II and today forms the lower part of the famous St.
Stephen's Crown.

The coronation of Géza with the crown received from
Michael Ducas probably took place in 1075.[29] Géza I, as
king of Hungary, lived only two more years after his eleva-
tion to the throne with Byzantine recognition and assistance.
After Géza's death in 1077, his brother Ladislas was invited by the majority of the Hungarian nobles to occupy
the throne. This was in violation of the rights of the lawful
king, Salomon, who was then holding out in the fortress
of Pozsony (Pressburg).[30] Ladislas tried to come to terms
with him, and since Henry IV, momentarily engaged in his
desperate struggle with Pope Gregory VII, could not give
much aid, Salomon seemed disposed to negotiate. In 1080
he resigned the Hungarian throne and went into voluntary
retirement, but secretly continued to form plots against
Ladislas. When these were discovered, Ladislas imprisoned
him near the royal castle of Visegrad.

The bitter struggle between the emperor and the pope
over lay investiture also influenced the attitude of Ladislas
towards the papacy. Ladislas' wife, Adelheid, was daughter
of Rudolf, duke of Swabia, who after the excommunication
of Henry IV in 1077 was elected king of Germany by the
German princes. Although Ladislas did not intervene in
favor of his father-in-law in the ensuing civil war in Germany, the pope nevertheless considered Ladislas a potential
ally against Henry IV. In a letter in which Ladislas was
admonished to receive the papal legates, Pope Gregory VII
addressed Ladislas as elected king of Hungary and thereby
gave him formal recognition without asking him to recognize the overlordship of the Holy See over Hungary.[31]

After the removal of Salomon from the scene, Ladislas
was also able to reinforce his position within the country.

Salomon, this restless and romantic member of the Arpád dynasty, was released from prison on the occasion of the canonization of Stephen, the first king. He eventually went into exile and, after the death of his German wife, married the daughter of the ruler of the nomadic Cumans. He lost his life fighting for the Cumans against the Emperor Alexius I Comnenus.[32]

In his foreign policy Ladislas also laid the foundations of a close relationship between Hungary and Croatia which was to last more than eight hundred years and which gave a new, southwestern direction to Hungarian expansion. As a result of this expansion, the Dalmatian coast of the Adriatic was to become in the next century a new point of friction between the Byzantine Empire and Hungary.

During the reign of Michael VII Ducas the weakening of Byzantine military power encouraged the aspirations toward independence of the Slavs in the Balkans and in the Adriatic provinces of the empire. First, a revolt broke out in 1072 among the Bulgarians, who were instigated by Michael Bogislav, Serbian grand-zupan, or prince, of the semi-independent principality of Zeta (the former Dioclea, present-day Montenegro). Michael sent his son, Constantine Bodin, to the Bulgarians, who proclaimed him tsar in Prizren.[33] It was with great difficulty that the revolt was quelled by the Byzantine armies, but the situation in the Adriatic theme of Dalmatia, which included the Adriatic coast with the towns of Zara and Ragusa, still remained unclear.[34]

While Dalmatia, the Adriatic coast, had formed a regular theme of the empire since the time of Basil II, the adjoining inland districts of Dioclea, Rascia, and Bosnia, and Croatia in the extreme northwest, were not organized as themes but, under their native rulers, formed Byzantine vassal principalities.[35] The Croatian prince, or zupan, Peter Cresimir, around the time of the Bulgarian revolt of Constantine Bodin extended his possessions at the expense of the Dalmatian theme, profiting from the difficulties of Michael VII Ducas in the Balkans. His successor, Zvonimir (1074-1088), went even further and exchanged the suzerainty of the Byzantine emperor for that of the pope. In 1075 or 1076 at Spalato he was crowned king by two apostolic legates of Pope Gregory VII and he recognized himself as a papal vassal. Two years later, in 1077, Michael Bogislav, the prince of Zeta (Dioclea), also received a royal crown from the pope and entered into the vassalage of the Holy See.[36]

The coronation of Zvonimir was an important turning point in the history of Croatia because it also marked the beginning of closer relations with the kingdom of Hungary. King Ladislas of Hungary, who endeavored to strengthen his position by family ties with foreign dynasties, gave his sister Helen (Ilona) in marriage to Zvonimir. When internal strife broke out in Croatia following the death of Zvonimir in 1088 without male heir, Ladislas intervened to protect the rights of his sister, and placed Croatia under Hungarian occupation. He entrusted the governorship of the country to his nephew Prince Almos, Géza I's son, who later was to play an important, if rather unfortunate, role in Byzantine-Hungarian relations.[37]

Before Ladislas could complete the occupation of Croatia and extend it to the Adriatic coast, however, he was interrupted by a Cuman invasion of southern Hungary and forced to turn his main forces against this new enemy. Thus only the northern part of Croatia remained under Hungarian control.

Toward the end of his reign, probably in 1090 or 1091, Ladislas also started a policy of reconciliation with Germany and the Emperor Henry IV, and refused to yield to the requests of Pope Urban II on the question of lay investiture. It seems that Ladislas in the last years of his reign was regarded by Pope Urban II as supporter of the schismatic party of the anti-pope Clement III, who had been elected in 1080 by the German bishops in defiance of Gregory VII. Certainly a change is evident in the attitude of the papacy toward Ladislas, who at the beginning of his reign was given unrestricted recognition by Gregory VII. This is clear from a letter which Pope Urban II addressed shortly after Ladislas' death to his successor, Coloman. Although this letter was probably written right after Ladislas' death in June, 1095, not a single word refers to him. Instead, it exhorts Coloman to follow the leadership of St. Peter's successors and not to be misled by Guibertus (Clement III), head of the heretics.[38]

Ladislas on the whole seems to have followed his predecessor's foreign policy, balancing East against West without attaching himself completely to either one, and preserving a neutral attitude in the investiture struggle between the papacy and the German emperor.

Ladislas had no male heir. The next relatives in the male line of the Arpád dynasty were his nephews Coloman and Almos, both sons of Géza I. Ladislas seems to have favored the younger brother, Almos, whom he appointed governor, or viceroy, of the occupied Croatian territories. This apparently hurt the feelings of the elder brother, Coloman, who during Ladislas' reign went in self-imposed exile to Poland. It was from there that Ladislas, during the last part of his reign, recalled him and designated him as legitimate heir of the Hungarian throne.

Coloman ascended the throne in 1095, a man in his twenties, physically unattractive but exceptionally erudite. There are two important documents from the time of his accession to the throne. One is the letter of Pope Urban II addressed to "Columbanus, king of the Hungarians," which, as we have mentioned, fails rather significantly to mention Ladislas. The other document is a letter of the Emperor

Henry IV sent to Almos, asking him to intervene with his brother, the new king, in order to preserve the good relations between the empire and Hungary which were restored under Ladislas.[39]

The friendly tone of the second letter indicates that Henry was fully confident of the attitude of Almoş toward him and that Coloman apparently had the reputation of being more understanding to the papal position in the investiture struggle than Ladislas had been.[40] Indeed, Coloman's foreign policy represents a departure from the independent policy of balance maintained by his two predecessors, Géza I and Ladislas, who sought to maintain good relations with both the German and Byzantine empires and to stay aloof in the investiture struggle.

At the very beginning of his reign, Coloman was confronted by the passage of the crusaders, who marched through Hungary on their way to the Holy Land. He had to fight against the first wave, the undisciplined "Peoples Crusade," but the main force, under the command of Godfrey of Bouillon, gained free passage through Hungary without serious incident.[41] As soon as this danger passed, Coloman concentrated on resuming the conquest of Croatia and extending Hungarian control to the Adriatic coast. The time was particularly convenient for such a move since the Emperor Alexius I had to turn all his attention towards the problems which arose from the First Crusade.

While the Hungarian move in Dalmatia openly violated Byzantine suzerainty, Coloman's marriage to a Norman princess, the niece of Robert Guiscard, indicated a rapprochement with the Normans, who represented a constant threat for the empire in the Adriatic area. This alienation of Hungary from Byzantium was somewhat counteracted by the marriage of Ladislas' daughter with John Comnenus, son of Alexius I. Yet, since the new family ties between the Comnenian dynasty and the Arpáds gave the Byzantine

the Croatian seacoast and in 1097 the Hungarians got a foothold at Zaravecchia (Biograd), near the important town of Zara. After the capture of Zaravecchia by the Hungarians, the Dalmatian cities solicited the protection of the doge of Venice, but Coloman shrewdly did not press the matter of conquest for the moment and concluded a treaty of non-aggression with the republic. It was at Zaravecchia, in May, 1097, that Coloman welcomed his future bride, who arrived there with an escort of Norman ships. From the marriage of Coloman with Busilla two sons were born, Ladislas, who died at an early age, and Stephen, who was to succeed Coloman on the throne.[1]

While Coloman sought to avoid a conflict with Venice, his diplomacy marks a significant abandonment of the neutralist policies of Ladislas and Géza I. The more intimate Hungarian-Norman relations not only placed Hungary in a stronger position against the Byzantine Empire, but since the Normans from the time of Robert Guiscard had been strong supporters of the papacy, with the Norman alliance the Hungarians apparently gave up their former neutral attitude in the investiture dispute and aligned themselves on the pope's side against the German emperor. This change was also reflected in Coloman's ecclesiastical policy within Hungary itself.[2]

In 1102 Coloman continued his expansion on the Adriatic coast with the occupation of the important city of Zara. From here the Hungarians conquered one by one the other Dalmatian cities, Traù, Spalato, and Ragusa. In Spalato they met the strongest resistance, but the conquest in general was made relatively easy by the failure of the Dalmatian cities to unite for a common defense. Afterwards, Coloman allowed them to retain their former autonomy. This lenient attitude disarmed much of the opposition against him.[3] Pope Pascal II acknowledged the conquest by sending Cardinal Augustinus to Coloman as papal legate for

Hungary and Dalmatia.[4] Thus Coloman's new title, "King of Croatia and Dalmatia," which he had been using since 1102, gained official recognition thanks to his pro-papal policy.

Coloman's conquests, and probably also his pro-papal policy, aroused the jealousy of the German Emperor Henry V, who for his own part made certain claims to the occupied territories. In fact, in 1108 he started a campaign against Hungary, supporting the interests of Prince Almos, the rebellious younger brother of Coloman. This intervention, however, was repelled by Coloman right at the border of Hungary.[5] It is surprising that besides the rather feeble attempt of Venice to relieve Zara, Henry's move was the only serious international reaction to the Hungarian penetration of the Adriatic area. The reason for this lay obviously in the fact that around the turn of the twelfth century the major powers on the Adriatic, Byzantium and the Normans, were heavily engaged in the affairs of the First Crusade, and even more in a subsequent struggle between Alexius Comnenus and Bohemond, son of Robert Guiscard, for the possession of Antioch. Furthermore, Coloman's marriage with the Norman Busilla secured him the tacit consent of the Normans for his action in Dalmatia. All these circumstances gave Coloman considerable freedom of action in the Adriatic area.

The reaction of Byzantium to Coloman's expansionist moves was relatively mild. This can be explained, if we examine Byzantine policies at the turn of the century. Alexius I Comnenus, founder of the Comnenian dynasty, ascended the throne of Byzantium in 1081 under unusually difficult circumstances. Many years of anarchy and civil wars had preceded his accession. At the beginning of his reign the whole of Asia Minor was practically lost to the Turks. In the West, Robert Guiscard had eliminated the Byzantine presence in southern Italy, and had subsequently turned against the eastern coast of the Adriatic, perhaps with the ultimate aim of obtaining the imperial crown of Byzantium.

Alexius, an intelligent, astute, and determined statesman and administrator, a great general and shrewd diplomat, restored the enfeebled imperial authority, and put an end to civil wars. In the face of the Norman danger he secured an alliance with the Venetian republic in a treaty concluded in 1082. The predominant position of Venice on the Adriatic was also threatened by the growing Norman power. The republic, therefore, was ready to offer her naval support to the empire in return for extraordinary trade privileges granted to the Venetians by the Byzantine government. Although the Venetian fleet inflicted a serious defeat on the Norman ships which attacked Dyrrhachium (Durazzo), this Byzantine stronghold on the eastern Adriatic shore was nevertheless taken by the Normans, and during the first years of his reign, Alexius was forced to wage a defensive war against the Normans in Epirus and Thessaly. The imminent danger was averted in 1085, at least temporarily, by the sudden death of Robert Guiscard and by the ensuing rivalry between his sons Roger and Bohemond.[6]

As has already been indicated in the previous chapter, with the pontificate of Gregory VII the papacy began to play an increasingly active diplomatic role and this was reflected in Byzantine-papal relations. In 1073-74 an intensive correspondence developed between Pope Gregory VII and the Emperor Michael VII Ducas concerning a possible reunion of the Eastern and Western Churches. The emperor, in turn, asked for western military aid against the Seljuk Turks. This aid, as the pope conceived it, would have taken the form of a great European crusade.[7]

During the negotiations Michael VII also asked the pope to mediate between Byzantium and the Normans, who in 1071 had captured the last Byzantine possessions in southern Italy. Robert Guiscard, the Norman leader, finally agreed to make peace with Byzantium; his daughter was to be married to Michael's son. This agreement, however, was ended in 1078 by the palace revolution in Constantinople which dethroned Michael VII. The new emperor, Nicephorus Botaniates, imprisoned Michael's son and canceled the marriage project with the Norman princess.

Robert Guiscard thereupon decided to invade Byzantine territory in the Balkans under the pretext of restoring the dethroned Emperor Michael. He succeeded in convincing Pope Gregory VII of the righteousness of his cause and the pope excommunicated the new emperor. Moreover, when Nicephorus himself abdicated and was succeeded in 1081 by Alexius Comnenus, Pope Gregory VII excommunicated Alexius too.

Such was the situation at the time of the Norman aggression during the first years of Alexius I's reign. After the deaths of Robert Guiscard and Pope Gregory VII, however, which both occurred in the same year, 1085, things changed. With the election of Pope Urban II in 1088 following the brief pontificate of Victor III, relations between the papacy and the Byzantine Empire improved considerably and negotiations were opened between the pope and Alexius. Urban II relieved the emperor from the excommunication, while Alexius proposed to hold an ecumenical council in Constantinople to eliminate the differences between the Eastern and Western Churches which was to be attended either by a papal delegate or by the pope himself.[8]

It was in this spirit of reconciliation between Rome and Byzantium that Pope Urban II issued his famous appeal for a crusade at the Council of Clermont in 1095. Yet the First Crusade only intensified the already existing antagonism between the Greeks and the Latins and Franks of the West. Alexius, who had expected the West to send him only a small expeditionary force, was alarmed by the presence

of four sizable armies and especially disturbed to see among
the leaders Bohemond, the son of his former enemy Robert
Guiscard. Soon the latent hostility between the Byzantines
and the Normans broke into the open.

Bohemond, like most of the Latin princes, had sworn
an oath to return the recaptured cities of Asia Minor to
the Byzantine emperor. Yet, after the capture of Antioch
in 1098, he refused to turn the city over to the Byzantines.
Alexius immediately sent an army against him, while Bohemond accused Alexius of having failed to assist the crusaders
in their struggle for possession of Antioch, thereby forfeit-
ing his claims to the city.[9] The Normans also blamed the
emperor for the failure of the crusade of 1101. In 1104
Bohemond entrusted his nephew Tancred with the command
of Antioch and himself returned to Italy. His primary
purpose was to raise a new army. He also visited France
and everywhere spread the idea that Alexius had betrayed
the cause of the crusaders.[10] In 1107 he returned to the
Balkans and laid siege to Dyrrhachium, but Alexius' superior strategy forced him to capitulate. Following this defeat,
Bohemond recognized Byzantine suzerainty over Antioch
in the treaty of 1108. The treaty, however, was never
carried out because Tancred refused to deliver Antioch to
the emperor. Bohemond died in 1111 and Alexius was
unable to organize an alliance of the Frankish princes
against Tancred.[11]

It is against this background that Alexius' passive attitude in regard to Hungarian expansion in Dalmatia should
be examined. Recognizing the growing influence of Hungary
in the Balkans and the danger which might result from
Hungarian-Norman cooperation on the Adriatic, Alexius
with his usual flexible diplomacy endeavored to disrupt the
alliance which was already in the making between Hungary
and the Normans. Since a Byzantine counterattack against
Hungary in the Balkans or in Dalmatia would have only

strengthened these ties, Alexius decided to counterbalance them by establishing a closer family relationship with the dynasty of Arpád through a diplomatic marriage. It was probably during the last conflict with Bohemond that the Byzantine court started negotiations with Coloman to obtain his consent to the marriage of his cousin Piroska, daughter of the late king Ladislas, with Alexius' son John, presumptive heir to the throne; at least it is around this time that closer relations between Hungary and the Byzantine court are noticeable. According to Anna Comnena, it was at the peace negotiations with Bohemond in 1108 that two Hungarian noblemen, Peter and Simon, participated as special envoys of the Hungarian king.[12]

The marriage of John and Piroska took place around 1108. The Hungarian princess embraced the Orthodox faith, changed her name to Irene, and later became empress of Byzantium beside her husband John Comnenus. They had eight children, among them the future emperor, Manuel. As empress Piroska-Irene took a lively interest in her husband's magnificent religious foundations, among them the monastery of Pantokrator. She was highly praised for her pious activities by Cinnamus, who regarded her as the actual founder of the monastery.[13] The marriage of John Comnenus with Irene was to become the source of further Byzantine-Hungarian connections, especially when Hungary was plunged into a period of succession disputes after Coloman's death.

Besides the conquest of Dalmatia and the recently established family ties between the Byzantine and Hungarian dynasties, a third development during Coloman's reign had, from the Byzantine point of view, particular interest. This was his conflict with his younger brother, Prince Almos. Almos, who during Ladislas' reign had represented the authority of the Hungarian king in Croatia, had been removed from his post by Coloman. This was probably owing to the fact that Coloman had been bypassed by Ladislas, whose favorite nephew Almos was. It is also possible that the friendship which apparently existed between Almos and the Emperor Henry IV made Coloman concerned for his own good relations with the papacy. At any rate, it was now Almos' turn to be pushed into the background. Disappointed, he first sought the support of Henry IV, and after the abdication of the latter he visited the court of Boleslav III, the duke of Poland. The latter became his brother-in-law in 1104 when Almos married Predslava, the daughter of Svyatopolk II, grand price of Kiev.[14] These moves perhaps already reflect his aims to remove Coloman from the throne.

A few years later Almos again appeared in Germany and apparently succeeded in persuading the new emperor, Henry V, to support him against Coloman. Henry, perhaps concerned by Hungary's new pro-papal policy and Dalmatian expansion, actually started an armed intervention in favor of the Hungarian royal pretender. This intervention, as we mentioned before, was unsuccessful; the German army was repelled at the western borders of Hungary. Almos next made a pilgrimage to the Holy Land and upon his return in 1113, asked and obtained his brother's forgiveness. In order to prove his good intentions, Almos founded a monastery, and his reconciliation with the king was seemingly complete.[15] After the birth of his son, however, Almos again resumed his intrigues, and ultimately the indulgence which Coloman had shown toward his brother until then began to diminish.

This change in the king's attitude was probably also caused by the misfortune which beset his family. Coloman's first wife, Busilla, died in 1112. His second marriage, with Euphemia, daughter of Vladimir II Monomach, prince of Smolensk and later grand prince of Kiev, was unfortunate; Coloman accused her of adultery and in 1113 sent her back

to Russia, where she bore an illegitimate son, Boris, whom
he repudiated.[16] At this time Coloman had only one son,
Stephen, by his first wife. Another son born by Busilla had
died in infancy.

After his unfortunate second marriage Coloman became
extremely fearful of his brother, whom he suspected, perhaps not without reason, of a desire to secure the succession
for his own son, the infant Béla. Whether Coloman had
actual proof against Almos is not known. The chronicle
of Otto von Freising relates only that Coloman, shortly
before his death in February, 1115, had Almos and his
young son captured and blinded.[17]

Coloman's action, which by its extreme cruelty reminds
us of the methods of the Byzantine court in dealing with
inconvenient rivals and pretenders, not only threw a dark
shadow on the memory of the great king, but had various
repercussions abroad. Almos sought refuge in Constantinople at the court of Alexius Comnenus and after Alexius'
death enjoyed the hospitality of the Emperor John Comnenus, whose wife Irene was his first cousin. Meanwhile,
Almos' son, the little Béla, was left behind in Hungary in
the custody of the Benedictine monastery of Pécsvárad,
where he spent several years hidden from his enemies in
the royal court.[18]

Almos, who changed his name to Constantine while in
exile, was offered a comfortable place of retirement in
Macedonia, where a considerable number of his Hungarian
followers gathered around him, forming there a group of
political refugees. Besides the sympathy which the empress
must have felt towards her unfortunate cousin, the presence
of a Hungarian exile colony in the empire gave a definitely
political character to the asylum granted Almos. The presence of a potential Hungarian royal pretender at the
Byzantine court was probably welcomed by the emperor;
in the event of a conflict between the empire and Hungary

such a person could serve as a valuable asset and weapon against the actual occupant of the Hungarian throne.[19]

For the time being, however, the possibility of such conflict was remote. The weakening of the royal authority in Hungary after Coloman's death in 1115 prevented any expansionist moves. Coloman's only son, Stephen II, was only fifteen years of age when he ascended the throne. Previously he had lost both his mother and his father and his education had probably been left to some Norman noblemen who belonged to the suite of Queen Busilla.[20] His adventurous, turbulent, unstable character made him more fit for the role of wandering knight than of Hungarian king.

Upon receiving news of Coloman's death the Venetians promptly attacked the Dalmatian cities. In this campaign Byzantine troops actively participated on the side of Venice, and the Dalmatian cities, one after the other, opened their gates to the Venetians.[21] In 1117 a Hungarian army appeared before the walls of Zara, and in the ensuing battle the doge, who personally conducted the defense of the city, lost his life. Nevertheless, the lack of strong leadership among the Hungarians made the attempt to recover Dalmatia unsuccessful. A truce probably followed between Hungary and Venice, because until 1124 the cities remained under unchallenged Venetian control.[22]

In that year Stephen II, already aged twenty-four, led an army to recover Dalmatia. By this time the Dalmatian cities were apparently dissatisfied with Venetian rule and welcomed the Hungarian intervention.[23] In retaliation the Venetians completely destroyed Zaravecchia, the oldest Hungarian coastal stronghold. In spite of the friendly attitude of the population, Stephen was unable to recover the Dalmatian cities, and during his lifetime the seacoast remained securely under Venetian control. From 1125 until his death in 1131, Stephen, despite some minor conflicts with Polish and Russian princes and with Luitpold, the markgraf of Austria, concentrated his forces against the Byzantine Empire.

The campaigns of Stephen II coincided with the reign of John Comnenus, who succeeded Alexius in 1118. John not only continued Alexius' work, the reconstruction of Byzantine power and recovery of the lost territories in Asia Minor, but also turned his interest toward the West. It is with him that there appeared for the first time in the Comnenian period the idea of restoring the ancient splendor of the Empire. This idea in large measure determined the policies of his son and successor, Manuel.

In the European peripheral spheres of the empire there were three major areas where imperial foreign policy left the defensive stage and took a more aggressive character under John Comnenus. One such area was the Adriatic and Dalmatia. Here, in the false belief that with the death of Bohemond the Norman danger had passed, John tried to reduce the excessive advantages which Venetian trade had enjoyed since the time of Alexius and which were justified only by the important anti-Norman alliance with Venice. When the Doge Domenico Michieli requested renewal of the commercial treaty and trade privileges in 1122, John refused. This was considered a hostile act by Venice and in the same year her fleet directed several attacks against Byzantine possessions in the Aegean archipelago. Since the empire did not have sufficient naval forces, John ultimately was forced to sign a new treaty in 1126 which confirmed the republic's earlier commercial privileges.[24]

On the Adriatic coast it was evident that John Comnenus was not prepared to tolerate Hungarian penetration into a Byzantine sphere of interest without taking some counter-measures. The war with the Venetian Republic, former guardian of Byzantine interests in Dalmatia, and the lack of Byzantine naval power, however, prevented the emperor from carrying out such action against Hungary in Dalmatia. The center of gravity in Byzantine-Hungarian relations during his reign therefore shifted from the Adriatic coast to the Danube frontier and the Balkans, Byzantium's second major sphere of interest in Europe.

In the Balkans the empire took the offensive, and in 1122 the Pechenegs, who once more invaded and plundered Thrace and Macedonia, were crushed and permanently liquidated. They never again recovered from this annihilating defeat and disappeared as a people from the stage of history.[25] Subsequently Byzantium suppressed a revolt of the Serbian zupan of Rascia. The Serbians again had to acknowledge imperial overlordship, but in their subsequent bids for independence found a new ally in the Hungarian kingdom, which in the first half of the twelfth century began to consolidate her position in the Balkans and, as will be discussed later, established close relations with Rascia.[26]

The third area where Byzantine interests were closely affected, was southern Italy. Here, in the earlier part of John's reign, in Sicily as well as in Apulia and Calabria, the inheritance of both Roger I and Robert Guiscard fell into the hands of inexperienced young rulers who at least temporarily diminished the Norman threat to the empire.

Things changed, however, after the death of Robert Guiscard's grandson, William, prince of Apulia, for William's cousin, Roger II, count of Sicily, profited by the temporary interregnum in Apulia and Calabria and occupied Salerno, Amalfi, Benevento, and Troia, receiving the homage and recognition of the local nobility. In 1127 he united under his authority Sicily and the Norman possessions on the mainland.

Pope Honorius II tried to reassert papal suzerainty over Apulia against Roger, but his efforts remained unsuccessful, for at the same time the rivalry of two major Roman families, the Pierleoni and the Frangepani, made the pope's position rather precarious. Roger even succeeded in imposing his authority over Capua. When Pope Honorius II finally died, the rivalry of the two powerful families led to a papal schism and to the simultaneous election of two popes, Innocent II and Anacletus II. In 1130 the latter, soon regarded as anti-pope, recognized Roger II as king of the united kingdom of Sicily, Calabria, and Apulia.[27]

The unification of Sicily and southern Italy under Roger II was a heavy blow to the Byzantine Empire, which had not yet given up its claims to the lost possessions in southern Italy. Against this renewed Norman danger, John Comnenus sought a rapprochement with the German emperor, Lothar II. In contrast to his predecessors, Lothar was a faithful supporter of the papacy and in several campaigns had helped Pope Honorius II and his legitimate successor, Innocent II, against the Normans and the anti-pope Anacletus II. After Lothar's death, John Comnenus, in order to consolidate Byzantine-German cooperation in Italy, also solicited the friendship of Lothar's successor, the first Hohenstaufen, Conrad III. Their alliance was sealed in 1142 by the engagement of John's son Manuel to a German lady of royal blood, Bertha of Sulzbach, the sister of Conrad's wife.[28]

The new Byzantine policy of rapprochement with the western empire inaugurated by John Comnenus (1118-1143) inevitably threatened the traditional Hungarian policy of balance between the Byzantine and German states. Hungary was now facing the danger of encirclement by her two powerful neighbors. It would seem that John Comnenus wanted to apply towards Hungary the same policy which had been persistently followed by the Byzantine emperors with regard to the Serbian princes of Rascia and Zeta (Dioclea), i.e., to keep always at their disposal an exiled prince from among the competing pretenders and to play him against a disobedient ruler who failed to fall into line with the imperial policies.

John Comnenus had every reason to be discontented with Stephen II's attitude because of his recent attempt to reconquer Dalmatia. Presumably this was the reason why the emperor brushed aside Stephen's protests against the sheltering of his rival, the blind Prince Almos.[29] The latter meanwhile was also joined in his Macedonian retreat by his young son, Prince Béla.

Hostilities between Byzantium and Hungary soon ensued over alleged mistreatment of Hungarian merchants at the Byzantine border stronghold of Branicevo on the Danube. It is, however, more likely that the real cause of the conflict was the resentment which Stephen felt on account of the political asylum granted his blinded uncle and his followers by the Constantinople government.[30] Hungarian sources mention, as possible reason, a rumor which had probably been spread by the Hungarian court in order to gain popular support for the action. It was alleged that the king had been forced to go to war against the Byzantine emperor because the latter had offended his wife, the Hungarian-born empress, when she protested against the emperor's decision to extend his overlordship over Hungary. According to these sources Stephen was asked to intervene by the empress herself.[31]

Stephen started his Greek campaign with an attack on Branicevo in 1127 or 1128. According to Nicetas Choniates, the Hungarians conquered and destroyed the stronghold and penetrated deeply into Byzantine territory along the valleys of the Morava and the Maritza, taking Niš and ravaging Sophia and the environs of Philippopolis.[32] The other Byzantine source, Cinnamus, places the first Hungarian attack at Belgrade, which was destroyed and its stones transported by the Hungarians to the opposite bank of the Danube and used there in the construction of the fortress of Semlin (Zemun).[33] It was probably in the spring of the following year that John Comnenus set out from his headquarters at Philippopolis, and the Byzantine army, supported by the imperial flotilla on the Danube, reached the Hungarian borders at Haram, where the river Nera meets the Danube. This place, called Χραμόν by Nicetas and Cinnamus, is the present-day Nova Palanka.

After a fierce battle the Byzantine army crossed the Danube, conquered the Hungarian stronghold of Haram, and inflicted a severe defeat on Stephen's army at the river Karas, a northern tributary of the Danube. Following this victory the Byzantines reconquered Branicevo. According to Nicetas, they also occupied Semlin and the eastern extremity of the territory between the Sava and the Danube rivers, called "Francochorion," actually the vicinity of the onetime imperial seat, Sirmium, which since the time of Andrew I (1059) had been in the possession of Hungary.[34]

For the rest of the campaign Cinnamus is the only source. According to his narrative, the emperor returned to Constantinople, leaving behind a garrison at Branicevo which was then overpowered by the Hungarians. John was forced to return to the Danube border and retook Branicevo. But apparently his forces were insufficient, because when an Italian woman who was a spy in the Hungarian court reported that Stephen was approaching with an army to make a surprise attack, John beat a hasty retreat, even leaving behind part of his equipment. Shortly after this event a peace treaty was concluded between John and Stephen, but about its details the Byzantine and Hungarian sources remain silent. Apparently it did not contain any territorial changes.[35]

It is very probable that the restoration of peace was partly the consequence of the death of Prince Almos. He died in Macedonia during the war, around 1129. Several years later, in 1137, when his son Béla succeeded Stephen

II on the throne, Almos' body was exhumed and transported
to Hungary.[36]

With Almos' death the interest of the Byzantine court
turned toward another Hungarian pretender, Boris, the
illegitimate son of Euphemia, Coloman's second wife. Boris
was born and raised in Kiev and during the reign of Stephen
II had already made an abortive attempt to acquire the
Hungarian crown. He had returned to Hungary and
formed a conspiracy against Stephen. The plot was discovered, however, and Boris fled to Constantinople.[37] According to Cinnamus and Otto of Freising, Boris then
married a princess of the imperial family.[38] This marriage
suggests the conclusion that John Comnenus, after the dis-
appearance of Almos from the scene, became interested in
having a new Hungarian pretender at his court, and thus
supported Boris' claims as long as Stephen II was on the
Hungarian throne. After Stephen's death, however, Almos'
son, the blind Béla II, ascended the throne of Hungary.
John apparently did not want to place difficulties in the way
of the son of a former protégé; Boris therefore left Constantinople. It was only during the reign of Manuel Comnenus that Boris reappeared in Constantinople, bringing
along his son, Constantine.[39]

Stephen II, whose dissolute life undermined his health,
died in his early thirties without having children. One of
his last acts was to recognize Almos' son, Béla, as lawful
heir to the Hungarian throne. At the same time he negotiated the marriage of the young prince with Helena,
daughter of Uros, the zupan of Rascia.[40]

As a consequence of this marriage, the accession of Béla
II (1131-1141) brought close political ties between Hungary and the Southern-Slav peoples of the Balkans. Since
Béla II was prevented by his blindness from exercising royal
authority, the queen and her brother, Belos, played important roles at the Hungarian court. Serbian influence at

the court became even stronger during the minority of Béla's successor, his son, Géza II, for the boy's guardianship was entrusted to his maternal uncle, Prince Belos.[41]

At the beginning of Béla's reign his wife took bloody vengeance against those responsible for blinding him. The massacre of numerous high ranking noblemen created the right atmosphere for a new attempt on the part of Boris, the persistent pretender, who appeared with Polish and Russian troops. His army advanced deeply into Hungary but was repelled, and during the rest of Béla's reign he made no other attempts to secure the throne.[42]

Following these incidents there was a gradual, cautious, and peaceful expansion of Hungarian influence in the north-western part of the Balkans, along the valleys of the rivers Drina and Bosna. Rascia, the territory between the Morava and the Drina, had been drawn into Hungary's orbit through the marriage of Uros' daughter with the Hungarian king. This center of Serbian resistance movements against the empire, by making common cause with Hungary, more easily escaped Byzantine influence than the rest of greater Serbia.

In spite of this slow penetration into an area which until then had been an undisputed Byzantine sphere of interest, relations between the empire and Hungary remained unimpaired during Béla's reign, for the imperial court was still well disposed towards him, a former protégé of the Byzantine emperor. On the other hand, Béla also established friendly relations with the German court and gave his daughter Sophia in marriage to Henry, son of Emperor Conrad III.[43]

The favorable foreign political situation enabled Béla II to extend his undisturbed suzerainty over Bosnia or Rama, which he may have received from Uros as dowry on the occasion of his marriage. It is certain that the title of *rex*

Ramae was among the titles of Béla II and that in 1137 he appointed his son Ladislas prince of Bosnia.[44]

The relative relaxation of Byzantine interest in the affairs of Rascia and Bosnia was probably also due to the fact that in the last years of his reign John Comnenus had been again heavily engaged in campaigns against the Turks in Asia Minor and also in various disputes with the Latin princes of Syria. These solicited the aid of Byzantium against the Turks but refused to submit themselves to imperial suzerainty. John tried to bring the Latin princes into submission by force of arms, and in 1142 led an army against Raymond of Poitiers, who had married Constance, the heiress of Antioch, and was thus in possession of this important city, claimed by the emperor.[45]

Amidst his preparations to intervene against Raymond and Fulk, the Latin king of Jerusalem, John was wounded by a poisoned arrow while hunting in Cilicia. He died in April, 1143. On his deathbed the emperor designated as successor his younger son, Manuel, who was with him in the camp and whom the troops acclaimed as their new *basileus*.[46]

Béla II had already died two years earlier, at the age of thirty-two, and was succeeded by his eleven-year-old son, Géza II (1141-1162). During Géza's minority, as has been mentioned, it was Prince Belos, his guardian, who had the decisive voice in Hungarian politics. Since 1142 Belos had been *ban* or viceroy of Croatia and Dalmatia, and since 1145 also held the supreme office of *comes palatinus,* thus being empowered to act as substitute for the king if the latter were absent or unable to exercise his royal authority. Belos proved himself a talented and wise statesman, and during his virtual regency the ties between Hungary and Serbia became even stronger. Moreover, Belos' brother Pervoslav was zupan of Rascia. Therefore, when a conflict broke out between the Serbs of Rascia and the Constantinople government, Hungarian assistance to the Serbs was a foregone conclusion.[47]

Thus, the southward expansion of Hungary, which started under Ladislas and Coloman with the conquest of Croatia and the Dalmatian coast and already had been of concern to Byzantium, created towards the end of John Comnenus' reign a new cause for alarm in the northwestern part of the Balkans in the form of the close cooperation between Hungary and Serbia. Ultimately it was this increasing rapprochement with the Serbs which involved Hungary in a series of conflicts with the Byzantine Empire during the reign of Manuel Comnenus and introduced a period of intensive Byzantine influence in Hungarian history.

CHAPTER III

Manuel's Western Policy and the Balkans

THE alliance between Hungary and Rascia, a vassal principality of Byzantium, was not merely an isolated move based on the relationship between the Hungarian and Serbian ruling families and serving primarily to enhance the cause of Serbian independence. Cooperation with the Serbs and other Slavonic peoples was also of particular importance from the point of view of Hungarian national interests. Since the last years of John Comnenus' reign the Byzantine-German rapprochement put Hungary in a rather precarious situation between her two powerful neighbors, the Byzantine and the German empires. Unable to follow her traditional policy of playing one great power against the other, Hungary apparently sought a way out through the formation of a large, independent Hungarian-Slavonic bloc centered in the Danube basin.

As was indicated earlier, the Serbs and Bulgarians had already revolted against Byzantium during the reign of Michael VII Ducas. The Bulgarian revolt was suppressed, but the Serbian zupan of Zeta (Dioclea), Michael Bogislav, had been able to preserve his independence, and in 1077 he was crowned king by the legates of Pope Gregory VII and became a vassal of the Holy See.[1] His son and successor, Constantine Bodin, succeeded in extending his authority, during the reign of Alexius Comnenus, from Zeta (present-day Montenegro) inland to Bosnia and Rascia (the region of which the center is Novi Bazar). After his death the

Emperor John Comnenus intervened in the struggle between Bodin's widow and the local zupans for Bodin's inheritance, and around 1123 Byzantine troops occupied Skadar (Scutari) and Cattaro, sending Bodin's widow, Jacquinta, as prisoner to Constantinople.[2] Bodin's son George, however, managed to escape to the mountains of Rascia, a region which has since remained the inaccessible stronghold of Serbian independence.[3]

Rascia gained new significance around 1130 when its zupan, Uros, gave his daughter in marriage to the Hungarian king, Béla II. Through these family ties Hungary gained control over one part of Serbian territory, the region called Bosnia or Rama, while at the same time the efforts of the Serbian zupans of Rascia to free their country from Byzantine control received Hungarian support.

This cooperation between Serbs and Hungarians in the twelfth century was the more significant from the point of view of Byzantium since both countries had formerly been in close contact with the Normans of southern Italy: Rascia under Bodin, whose father-in-law, Argyrus, was commander of the Norman and Lombard forces at Bari, and Hungary since the time of Coloman, who had married the daughter of Roger, the Norman duke of Sicily. The contacts between Hungary and the Norman-Sicilian kingdom were also maintained by Géza II, who sent his envoy, Adalbertus, to Roger II.[4] Unfortunately we do not possess any details of the results of this embassy. From the fact, however, that around the mid-twelfth century Norman-Sicily and Hungary were on friendly terms and were both enemies of Byzantium, and in addition since there had been close cooperation between Hungary and the Serbs, it seems probable that following the Second Crusade both Hungary and Serbia were interested in a coalition which Roger II, the king of Norman Sicily, tried to forge into a new crusade against Byzantium, possibly

with the participation of Pope Eugenius III and King
Louis VII of France.[5]
Thus, Hungarian expansion from the Danube basin into
the northwestern Balkans and the Serbian independence
movement both gained deeper significance during Manuel's
reign, mainly as aspects of a power combination which
intended to counteract the Byzantine emperor's plans to
extend his control over Italy and to restore in some form
the universalistic character of the eastern Roman, Byzantine Empire.

Manuel Comnenus, perhaps not the most talented, but
undoubtedly the most brilliant and complex personality of
the Comnenian dynasty, ascended the throne of Byzantium
in the fall of 1143. According to contemporaries, Manuel's
personal charm and tall, attractive stature gained him the
sympathy of everyone who came in personal contact with
him and inspired respect among his subjects.[6] Manuel
inherited the outstanding diplomatic and military abilities
of his father John II and his grandfather Alexius, and
these qualities were to serve him well as statesman and
commander. Yet he did not possess Alexius' calculating
shrewdness or John's clever, cold prudence.[7]

On his mother's side Manuel was descended from the
dynasty of the Arpáds. His maternal grandfather was
King Ladislas of Hungary, and it was perhaps his Hungarian ancestry which added a peculiar restlessness, a fiery
temperament, and an almost barbarian touch to his character. As a consequence of this temperament and of his
personal courage he often involved himself in dangerous
situations on the battlefield, and exposed himself to risks
unnecessary for a *basileus*.[8] His statesmanship far sur-
passed his military abilities and in the diplomatic field he
displayed unusual finesse, patience, and perseverance, but
in the long run his political concepts proved to be unreal-
istic, overambitious, almost utopian. It was as though his

personal inclination toward adventure also influenced his judgment of political situations.

In his private life Manuel abandoned the sober, austere moral principles which characterized the court of John II and Irene. He sought pleasures and gallant adventures, and with him the ideals and manners of western chivalry entered the rigid, formal atmosphere of the Byzantine court for the first time. Very soon after his first marriage to Bertha of Sulzbach, the sister-in-law of the German Emperor Conrad III, Manuel began a long succession of amorous adventures. Among his mistresses the name of only one is known to historians; this is his niece Theodora, probably the daughter of his sister Maria and of John Roger. Theodora bore him an illegitimate son and occupied an elevated position at the court as the emperor's official favorite.[9]

Although a model of the western *chevalier* and a lover of pleasure and luxury, Manuel was also a highly educated man who acquired considerable versatility and knowledge in such divergent intellectual fields as theology, literature, philosophy, astrology, and medicine. When Conrad III fell ill in Constantinople on his return from the Second Crusade, it was Manuel himself who provided medical treatment to the German emperor.[10]

The gradual infiltration of western elements into the life of Byzantium was in large part a natural consequence of the closer and more frequent contacts between Greeks and Latins which had developed since the First Crusade and had been deepened by the Second Crusade. But during Manuel's reign the admission of western influences appears to have been a conscious, deliberate effort on the part of the emperor and his government. By opening Byzantium to western influences, and by deliberately assimilating elements of Latin culture, Manuel attempted to modernize, to rejuvenate Byzantine society.

This rapprochement with the West was also in line with his general policy, which was a diversion of Byzantine interests toward southern Italy, and which, especially after the rupture between Pope Alexander III and the German Emperor Frederick I, seemed to aim ultimately at the restoration of the universal empire as it was in Justinian's time: a Roman empire with Constantinople as capital.[11] Thus the isolation of Byzantium, as it had existed since the iconoclast period of the eighth century, would cease and the assimilation of the Greek East to the Latin West, the merger of Byzantine civilization with Latin customs, culture, intellectual and religious life would enable Byzantium to establish its supremacy over the whole Christian world.

In general the main outlines of this ambitious scheme followed the policies of Alexius, and even more those of John II. John's leading idea had also been the restoration of the ancient splendor of the Roman empire. While Alexius and John, however, had to concentrate their efforts primarily on the recovery of the empire's strategic positions in the East, Manuel's western political orientation was dictated, not only by personal inclinations, but also by certain changes in the general political situation in western Europe, where the center of gravity had once more shifted to Italy and the Mediterranean.

The southern Italian scene had already started to become of first class importance for Byzantium under John II. As was pointed out earlier, the unification of Sicily with Apulia and Calabria under the scepter of Roger II in 1127 revived the Norman danger. And this had already prompted John II to turn his attention to the West and to seek an understanding with the German Emperor Lothar II, and later with Conrad III. Manuel's foreign policy therefore, at the beginning of his reign, appears to have been a direct continuation of his father's; and even the

main areas of Byzantine political activity in the West
remained the same—southern Italy, the Adriatic, and the
Danube frontier in the Balkans.

Whether Manuel's ultimate goal was the restoration
of the universal empire or merely the recovery of Byzantine possessions in southern Italy, the central area of his
western policy was southern Italy and the Adriatic. In
view of the friendly relations which existed since the time
of Coloman between Hungary and the Norman-Sicilian
kingdom, however, the area of the Balkans and the Danube
frontier also gained significance as a vulnerable northern
flank of the empire and as the shortest land route between
Byzantium and its German ally. The importance of this
Balkan frontier will be further demonstrated in connection with Manuel's campaigns against the Serbs and Hungarians.

Early in his reign Manuel's aim of building a common
front with Germany against the Normans was partly frustrated by the Second Crusade and the problem of Antioch.

In the East Manuel began by following his father's
aggressive policy aimed at pushing the Byzantine frontiers to the Euphrates and compelling the Armenian princes
of Cilicia and the Latin states of Syria to recognize his
suzerainty. Manuel perhaps wanted to assert Byzantine
supremacy even further south over the Mediterranean
coast and Palestine. His ambitions were indirectly supported by a resurgence of Turkish power, for in the face
of the Turkish menace the Latin princes solicited his aid.
Especially significant was the change in the attitude of
Raymond of Poitiers, the prince of Antioch. After the fall
of Edessa in 1144, Antioch was hard pressed by the Turks
and this prompted Raymond in 1145 to make a journey to
Constantinople and humiliate himself before the emperor,
asking his help against the Turks and to acknowledge
Byzantine suzerainty over Antioch.[12]

At the same time Manuel conducted two consecutive campaigns against the sultan of Iconium. In 1146 the Greek army reached the gates of Iconium, but for reasons which are not clearly explained by the historian of this campaign, Cinnamus, Manuel did not press the siege of the city. After having sacked the outskirts, the Byzantine army retreated. Presumably Manuel had received news of the approach of strong Turkish reinforcements.[13] In 1147 the news of an imminent new crusade made both Manuel and Sultan Mas'ud anxious to end hostilities, for the approach of the crusader armies of the West constituted a threat for both rulers. In the spring of 1147 a truce was negotiated which provided grounds for western accusations that Manuel had betrayed the cause of the crusade.[14]

Unquestionably, Manuel's actions with regard to the Turkish menace were less decisive than his father's. The prospect of a new crusade was perhaps partly responsible for this, but in any case Manuel's interests throughout this entire period remained concentrated on his western schemes, and the affairs of southern Italy, Serbia, and Hungary gained precedence over the Turkish problem.

As a consequence of the western orientation of his policy, Manuel's successes against the Turkish princes of Asia Minor were not convincing. He failed to take full advantage of the rivalries which existed between the various Turkish leaders and failed to destroy the power of the most dangerous among them, the sultan of Iconium. Following several minor Byzantine military successes, the sultan Kilidj Arslan did, however, offer a formal submission to Manuel in 1161 and promised to respect the imperial frontiers, as well as to furnish auxiliary troops at the emperor's request. In fact, according to Cinnamus, on one occasion Turkish auxiliaries fought in the ranks of the Byzantine army in a campaign against the Hungarians.[15]

For about a decade following this treaty with Kilidj
Arslan, Manuel was able to enjoy relative tranquillity
in the provinces of Asia Minor. Meanwhile, however, he
allowed the sultan enough time to fortify his position by
crushing rival Turkish leaders. When Manuel finally realized the danger and tried to resume an aggressive policy
against the Turks, his enemy in the East had grown too
strong and the Byzantine army suffered a disastrous defeat
at Myriocephalon in 1176.[16] Byzantine military power was
never able to recover completely from this disaster. Moreover, this defeat, occasioned in part by Manuel's western
preoccupations, also contributed to the ultimate failure of
his policy there.

Manuel's western policy, immediately after his accession
to the throne, showed a temporary deviation from the
political line of John Comnenus and in fact threatened
to disrupt the Byzantine-German alliance which John had
so carefully built up. It was under the shield of this
alliance, directed against the revived Norman danger from
Roger II, that John Comnenus had been able to initiate
his aggressive policy on the eastern borders of the empire.

Roger II, who assumed the title of king of Sicily and
united under his rule Sicily, Apulia, and Calabria, tried
to avert the dangers of the Byzantine-German alliance. He
offered direct negotiations to eliminate his differences with
the Byzantine Empire and by a special embassy requested
the hand of a Byzantine princess for one of his sons. Both
the attempted rapprochement and the marriage project
were, however, interrupted by the sudden death of John
Comnenus.[17]

It was in these circumstances that Manuel ascended the
throne in 1143 and encountered serious attempts to challenge his succession. Among those who opposed Manuel's
succession and tried to form a plot against him, were several Norman fugitives who had fled Sicily following the

revolts which introduced Roger II's reign. These fugitives, bitter enemies of Roger, entered into Byzantine service, and one among them, a certain John Roger, who had married an imperial princess, Maria, the daughter of John II, was thus even a member of the imperial family with the rank of *caesar*. The plot was discovered and the leaders, John Roger and another Norman nobleman, Robert, count of Capua, were arrested.[18]

Whether it was the ungrateful attitude displayed by the Norman refugees which prompted Manuel to resume the thread of reconciliation with Roger II, or simply because he wanted to maintain peaceful relations with Sicily until his throne was secure, we do not know. It might be also, as Chalandon suggests, that Manuel desired only to continue and bring to a conclusion the previous diplomatic negotiations which had been interrupted by John Comnenus' death.[19]

At any rate, a Byzantine ambassador, Basil Xeros, was sent to Palermo. According to Cinnamus, this ambassador was bribed by Roger II to conclude in Manuel's name a treaty extremely favorable to the Sicilian king. In this the Byzantine emperor was to recognize Roger as king of Sicily, a recognition which implied the renunciation of Byzantine claims in southern Italy. These negotiations and the treaty should probably be placed in the years 1143 or 1144.[20] It was obvious that the emperor could not accept this treaty and recognize the ruler of Sicily as an equal sovereign; indeed, Manuel repudiated the treaty and the ambassador who negotiated it fell into disgrace.[21]

After his unsuccessful attempt to bring about a *modus vivendi* with the Normans, Manuel had some difficulty in restoring the political line of his father, the Byzantine-German alliance. The news of negotiations between Manuel and Roger II had caused a serious strain in Byzantine-German relations. Conrad III was probably also irritated by the fact that, although the future bride had already spent her third year of waiting at the Byzantine court, the marriage between Bertha of Sulzbach and Manuel had not yet taken place.[22]

It was only in the spring of 1145, after protracted discussions between the Byzantine and German courts, that an agreement was finally ·reached. The new alliance was obviously directed against the Norman-Sicilian kingdom, which represented an equal danger for both empires. Conrad III, in view of the prospective family ties, promised, if necessary, to come to the aid of the Byzantine emperor with all his forces. The ́agreement was sealed by the marriage of Manuel and Bertha in January, 1146 during Manuel's campaign against the sultan of Iconium.[23]

If Manuel hoped the renewal of the alliance with Conrad would lead to a consolidation of the Byzantine position against the Normans, his hopes were frustrated in the next year by developments connected with the Second Crusade. The impetus for this crusade was given by the news of the fall of Edessa. The pleas of the Armenian bishops and of the emissaries of the Latin princes of Antioch and Jerusalem prompted Pope Eugenius III to issue a bull in December, 1145 calling for a new crusade. In March, 1146, Louis VII of France and a great number of the French nobility enrolled for the crusade. In December, 1146, Conrad III, under the impact of the eloquence of St. Bernard of Clairvaux, also decided to take the cross.

The prospect of a new crusade was highly unwelcome in Byzantium where the experiences of the First Crusade were still vivid enough in Greek memories, as well as in the pages of the *Alexiad,* to warn of the dangers which the presence of such a heterogeneous army would represent for the internal peace and security of the empire.[24] Above all it seemed obvious that the crusaders would necessarily bring reinforcements to the Latin states in Syria and thus make them less dependent on the support of the Byzantine emperor in their struggle against Islam. This meant that the successes of Manuel over the Latin princes, and particularly the submission of the prince of Antioch, would be jeopardized. Finally, the Normans, now relieved from the danger of German-Byzantine cooperation in Italy by Conrad's participation in. the crusade, were again a potential threat to the empire. Indeed, the value of the recently concluded alliance with the German emperor was substantially reduced by the crusade.[25]

This situation no doubt explains why Roger II was anxious to promote the cause of the crusade. He made an offer to Louis VII not only to transport the crusaders from Sicily to Syria by ship, but also to participate in the crusade. The offer was rejected and it was decided that the crusade would follow the land route of the First Crusade, passing through Hungary and the territories of the Byzantine Empire. The Norman alliance obviously seemed undesirable to Louis VII not only because of the antagonism which existed between Manuel and Roger, but also because the expansion of the Norman-Sicilian kingdom in southern Italy had alienated the pope, as well as the Emperor Conrad III, from Roger II. Moreover, Louis VII seemed to be aware that certain Norman designs on Syria and Palestine since the time of the First Crusade had earned the suspicion of the Latin princes of the East, particularly the prince of Antioch, Raymond of Poitiers, who was uncle of the French queen, Eleanor of Aquitaine.[26]

Thus, Hungary was to serve once more as territory of transit for the crusader armies of the West in their march toward the Balkans and the East. Louis VII entered into contact with Géza II asking for free passage and free purchase of supplies for the French crusaders. Géza sent a favorable reply and at the same time numerous Hungarians expressed their desire to join the crusader army.[27]

Conrad III and the German contingents left Nuremberg in May, 1147. At Regensburg the emperor met the envoys of Géza II, who demanded assurances that the crusaders, during their passage through Hungary, would not intervene in support of the pretender Boris.[28] This illegitimate son of Coloman reappeared at the German and French courts, soliciting the support of Conrad III and Louis VII, and declaring his intention of participating in the crusade.[29]

Apparently neither Conrad nor Louis were inclined to let the crusade get entangled with the succession problems of Hungary, and Géza II, after receiving the necessary assurances, granted free passage to the German crusader army when it reached the Hungarian border. During their passage the Germans showed a bellicose attitude as if they were in enemy territory and, according to the Hungarian sources, caused considerable damage to the population.[30] On the other hand, the French army which followed under the personal command of Louis VII maintained complete discipline. Boris entered Hungary together with the French crusaders and, when his presence became known, Géza II requested his extradition. The French king refused.[31] Apart from this incident contacts between Louis VII and Géza II remained friendly and the French army reached the Byzantine border at Branicevo without further incident.

While the crusader armies were still in Hungary, both Conrad and Louis received ambassadors from Manuel asking for assurances that the crusaders were coming as friends and that they would not endanger the security of the empire. In exchange Manuel promised free passage and a friendly reception in Byzantine territory. According to Cinnamus, both monarchs made solemn promises and confirmed these by oath. Thereupon the crusaders were transported across the Danube in Byzantine ships.[32] Manuel's main concern was to keep the crusader armies away from the capital. This he managed only after considerable difficulties and serious clashes between crusaders and Byzantine troops. New agreements were finally reached with both Conrad and Louis, and the French and German crusaders were transported across the Bosporus to Asia Minor.[33]

Meanwhile, Manuel's fears that the Normans would use this opportunity to attack the empire were fully realized. In the summer of 1147, while the crusader armies were approaching Constantinople, Roger II led an attack against the islands of Corfù and Euboea. The Normans entered the gulf of Corinth and besieged the city; they also landed on the Peloponnesus and occupied Thebes. From this city, which was a center of silk production, many skilled workers were deported to Palermo to strengthen the Sicilian silk industry.[34]

Since the main part of the Byzantine army was needed in the vicinity of the capital to control the passage of the crusaders, Manuel turned for aid to Venice. In September, 1147 new commercial privileges and concessions were granted to the republic. Venice in return placed her fleet on the Adriatic at the disposal of the Byzantine emperor till the end of 1148.[35]

Manuel was determined to retake Corfù, to bring the war to enemy territory, and ultimately to restore the authority of Byzantium in southern Italy. By the spring of 1148 a large army had been concentrated for this purpose in the Balkans and several hundred ships were also ready to begin operations when an unexpected event delayed the punitive action. While at Philippopolis on his way to the Adriatic coast with his army, Manuel received news of an invasion of the northern parts of the Balkans by the Cumans and was forced to turn first against these invaders.[36] Thus only the fleet, together with the Venetians, began the siege of Corfù.

After the Cumans were successfully repelled, the season

was so far advanced that Manuel was compelled to postpone the campaign against the Normans and lead his army
to a winter encampment. It was here, probably at Thessalonica, that Manuel received a visit from Conrad III.
After the disastrous failure of the crusade the German
emperor left Acre in September, 1148 and was already on
his way home. The two emperors proceeded to Constantinople where a new treaty was signed which secured for
Manuel full German support in the war against the Normans. Joint Byzantine-German action was supposed to start
in the next year and the treaty also provided for the parti-
tion of the territories to be conquered in Italy. Conrad,
probably convinced that alone he would be unable to destroy
the growing Norman power in Italy, renounced his claims
in the southern part of the peninsula and agreed that Apulia
and Calabria, after liberation from the Normans, should
be restored to the Byzantine Empire.[37]

In February, 1149 Conrad returned to Germany to pre-
pare for the projected campaign against Roger II. Meanwhile, the Byzantine fleet with the assistance of the Venetians resumed the siege of Corfù. Finally, in the summer
of 1149, Corfù opened its gates to Manuel and the emperor
moved his headquarters to Avlona on the eastern coast of
the Adriatic, to personally direct the transfer of Byzantine
troops to Italy. It was here that news of a revolt among
the Serbs reached him; he decided to remain in the Balkans
and subdue his rebellious vassals.

The Serbian revolt of 1149 seems not to have been an
isolated event. Rather it was one of the diplomatic ma-
neuvers of Roger II. Ever since the conclusion of the
alliance between Manuel and Conrad, Roger had sought to
counteract its effects by fomenting internal troubles within
Germany and, at the same time, by organizing a coalition
between the adversaries of the Byzantine emperor.

In Germany, Conrad's most serious rival, Henry the

Proud, the duke of Bavaria, had died in 1139, but his brother Welf, aided by Sicilian money, organized a revolt against Conrad when the emperor returned in 1149 from the crusade.[38] The revolt was suppressed, but the emperor was compelled to remain in Germany and to give up the projected invasion of Italy.

Apparently Roger also had a hand in the Serbian revolt which forced Manuel to turn his attention from the invasion of Italy to the Danube frontier. At least Cinnamus suggests that there was a connection between the projected expedition against Roger, the revolt in Germany, and the Hungarian-supported Serb revolt.[39]

But it was not only internal troubles which momentarily paralyzed both members of the anti-Norman alliance. Roger's diplomacy was also directed toward exploiting discontent in western Europe over the failure of the Second Crusade. People in the West blamed Manuel and the Byzantines for the disaster which befell the crusaders. Roger's schemes therefore included the organization of a new crusade, this time directed against Byzantium. In France such a plan was favored by the chief minister, Suger, and by public opinion. It was only Conrad's determination to remain true to the Byzantine alliance which frustrated Roger's schemes. It was obvious that without the participation of the German emperor a western crusade was not feasible.

Moreover, Pope Eugenius III had reservations about a crusade which would have primarily served Roger's interests. In fact, since the beginning of 1150 negotiations between the pope and Conrad led to a complete understanding concerning Conrad's prospective Italian expedition. This understanding had been furthered by the gradual deterioration of relations between the pope and Roger over the question of canonical freedom in episcopal elections and the admission of papal legates into southern Italy. Finally, in April, 1151, an open breach occurred when Roger, in repudiation of papal suzerainty, had his son William crowned at Palermo without the pope's consent.[40]

With good relations between the pope and the German emperor restored and the Byzantine-German alliance stronger than ever, it seemed in 1150 that nothing further stood in the way of Manuel's campaign against the Norman-Sicilian king except the Serbian revolt and the confused situation on the Danube frontier. It was therefore primarily in connection with Manuel's western political aims that the attitude of Hungary and her alliance with the Serbs gained exceptional significance.

Hungary's attitude became important not only because she supported the Serbian revolt which had temporarily delayed Manuel's action against the Normans, but much more because she stood on the direct land routes between Germany and Byzantium and thus could serve as either a connecting link or an obstacle to communications between the two empires. As long as these routes were controlled by a friendly power, they were much safer and shorter than the sea route from Byzantium to northern Italian ports continuously harrassed by the Norman fleet. It was, therefore, of paramount importance for Byzantine foreign policy to make sure that this vital land connection with Germany remained open and under control of a friendly government.

Thus, with the accession of Manuel, especially after the conclusion of his alliance with Conrad III, Hungary's geopolitical situation began to play an important role in Byzantine-German relations. The recognition of Byzantium's paramount interests in the Danube basin to a great extent determined Manuel's political and military moves during the major part of his reign. His preoccupation with Hungarian affairs had, as will be demonstrated later, adverse effects on the implementation of Byzantium's western political goals.

CHAPTER IV

Struggle for the Control of Hungary

THE rapprochement between the Byzantine and German empires during the reign of Conrad III not only revealed the strategic importance of Hungary from the point of view of Byzantium, but also created a new situation for Hungary and was largely responsible for a new turn of Hungarian policy marked by its Slavonic orientation.

The developments which led to this change go back before Manuel's reign and the Second Crusade to the time of John Comnenus, who had already aimed at securing Byzantine influence in Hungary by interfering in the Hungarian succession and by supporting the exiled pretenders of the Arpád dynasty. These efforts seemingly were successful, because after the death of Stephen II in 1131 the Hungarian throne had been occupied by Béla II (the Blind), son of an earlier pretender and protégé of the Byzantine court, Prince Almos-Constantine.

During Béla II's reign relations between Byzantium and Hungary remained correct. Yet it was Béla's marriage in 1130 or 1131 to the daughter of Uros, zupan of Rascia, which laid the foundations for a close and lasting cooperation between Hungary and the Serbian vassals of the Byzantine emperor.[1] And it was this marriage which opened the way for Serbian influence in the Hungarian court during the minority of Géza II, Béla's successor. The chief exponent of this policy was the *ban* and *comes palatinus,* Belos, son of the zupan of Rascia and brother of Helen, the dowager

queen of Hungary. It is with the accession of Géza II in
1141 that the outlines of a Hungarian-Slavonic bloc begin
to emerge.

The Slavonic orientation of Hungary, based primarily
on the family ties between the Hungarian and Serbian ruling
dynasties, was further strengthened in 1146 by the marriage
of Géza II to Euphrosyne, the daughter of Mstislav, grand
prince of Kiev, and granddaughter of Vladimir Monomach.[2]
Through this marriage Géza became involved in the rivalry
between Russian princes for the throne of Kiev. In 1150
he led an armed intervention in support of his brother-in-
law, Isiaslav, the prince of Pereyaslavl, against George
Dolgoruki, the prince of Suzdal. Isiaslav tried to liberate
Kievan Russia from both the political and religious influence of Byzantium and particularly to end the submission
of the metropolitan of Kiev to the patriarch of Constantinople.[3]

In the rivalry between Isiaslav and George Dolgoruki,
Manuel, in order to secure continued Byzantine influence in
Kiev, threw his support behind Dolgoruki and Vladimirko,
the prince of Halich, who allied himself with Dolgoruki
and was counted as a Byzantine vassal.[4] Thus, the actions
of the Hungarian king collided with the interests of Byzantium in Kievan Russia as well as in the Balkans.

From 1149 until the death of Isiaslav in 1154, Géza
repeatedly intervened in favor of his brother-in-law and
his campaigns necessarily brought him into conflict also with
Vladimirko, whose principality of Halich lay between Hungary and the territory of Kiev. In fact, because of the
Hungarian king's frequent campaigns, Russian chroniclers
called the road which led from Hungary through Sanok
and Przemysl toward Jaroslav and Vladimir the "royal
route."[5]

The close contacts of Hungary with Serbia and the principality of Kiev has prompted certain modern historians to

maintain that Hungary, which had already absorbed considerable Slavonic elements in Croatia and Dalmatia, was attempting around the mid-twelfth century to form a great Slavonic power-bloc between the German and the Byzantine empires.[6] It is enough to point to the racial and linguistic differences between the Hungarian and Slavonic peoples to make such a view highly questionable. On the other hand, it is true that during the reign of Géza II there was a definite tendency to strengthen already existing ties and to seek new contacts with the Slavonic peoples of eastern Europe. This new orientation, however, was not motivated by the desire to give a specifically Slavonic character to this new power-bloc, but was rather dictated by the necessity of finding new allies. This need arose because of a change in the attitude of Germany. Since the conclusion of the Byzantine-German alliance the traditional Hungarian policy of balance between Germany and Byzantium was no longer feasible.

At the beginning of Conrad III's reign, while Béla II occupied the throne of Hungary, relations between Hungary and the German Empire could be still considered as cordial. In 1139 Béla II's daughter, Sophia, was engaged to Prince Henry, Conrad's two-year-old son, and the Hungarian princess was sent to the German court to complete her education. Even after Béla's death, when Géza II succeeded his father on the throne, the government of Belos, the king's uncle and guardian, solicited at the German court the immigration of German settlers from the Rhineland to Transylvania, the eastern part of Hungary.[7]

A deterioration in German-Hungarian relations immediately followed the rapprochement of Byzantium with Germany under Conrad III. Conrad tacitly recognized Hungary as a Byzantine sphere of interest by carefully avoiding even a mention of Hungary in his correspondence with John Comnenus. In a letter dated February 12, 1142,

Conrad, in outlining the limits of his western *imperium,*
mentioned by name France, Spain, England, and Denmark
as adjoining kingdoms where Germany ha'd close political
interests and which were ready "to perform the commands"
imposed by the emperor. Hungary and the eastern neighbors
of Germany, however, are conspicuously missing from this
enumeration.[8]

German-Byzantine cooperation was also responsible for
Conrad's attitude towards Coloman's illegitimate son, Boris.
This constant and persistent pretender to the Hungarian
throne, who for some time enjoyed the hospitality and
support of the Byzantine emperor, in 1146 appeared in
Germany, trying to rally western support for his claims.
Conrad promised help to the protégé of Byzantium and did
not object when Boris, with the tacit consent of Henry of
Babenberg, duke of Bavaria and Austria, began to recruit
an army in the duke's territories.[9]

In September, 1146 the forces of Boris invaded Hungary and in a surprise attack captured the fortress of
Pozsony (Pressburg). Géza II immediately retaliated. Pozsony was retaken, and a strong army under the command
of the Ban Belos invaded Austrian territory. The main
encounter between the Hungarians and Henry's forces took
place near the border, along the river Fischa, and ended
with a complete defeat of the Germans; Henry himself
escaped only with difficulty from the battlefield and fled
toward Vienna.[10]

The Hungarians did not exploit their victory; the campaign had no continuation, possibly because of the news of
an imminent crusade.[11] The conflict did, however, have unfavorable repercussions on German-Hungarian relations and
resulted in the dissolution of the engagement of Conrad's
son to the Hungarian princess. The strained relations help
to explain the hostile attitude of the German crusader army
during its passage through Hungary one year later.

After the battle on the Fischa the Hungarians apparently discounted Germany as a possible ally against Byzantium. King Géza II and Belos turned with renewed interest toward their connections with Kiev and with the Serbs. This cooperation between Hungary and the principality of Kiev was also strengthened in 1150 by the engagement of Isiaslav's son Vladimir to the daughter of Belos.[12] Meanwhile, in 1148 the Byzantine-German friendship had been renewed at Constantinople and this new treaty of alliance was strengthened also by a marriage concluded between Theodora, Manuel's niece, and Henry of Babenberg, duke of Austria, the loser of the battle on the Fischa.[13]

Such was the international situation of Hungary in the mid-twelfth century, when the revolt of the Serbs in 1149 delayed Manuel's Italian expedition against Sicily. As has been indicated (p. 65), Cinnamus, not without reason, suspected Roger II's diplomacy of a role in the revolt of Manuel's Serbian vassals, who had been possibly encouraged by their Hungarian allies.[14] Rivalry among the Serbian leaders themselves also contributed to the confused situation in the Balkans. Two sons of the late Zupan Uros of Rascia, Pervoslav Uros, who held the position of zupan after his father's death, and Dessa, who later became better known in Serbian history as Stephen Nemanja, attacked the Zupan Radoslav of Zeta (Dioclea), a faithful vassal of the Byzantine emperor.

In 1149 Pervoslav and Dessa forced Radoslav to abandon the larger part of Zeta and to withdraw to the stronghold of Cattaro on the Adriatic coast. In this feud Pervoslav sought the aid of the third brother, Belos, who already held an important position at the Hungarian court as guardian of Géza II. Whether such aid was forthcoming cannot be stated definitely. The only contemporary source which indicates Hungarian intervention in this rebellion is the *Annals of Ipat*, which notes that in the year 1149 King

Géza II refused to send aid to his brother-in-law Isiaslav, claiming as excuse that he was at war against the Greeks.[15]

In the summer of 1149 Manuel assembled his troops at Avlona (Valona.), where they were waiting to be transported to Italy, and led them instead into the valley of the Morava to intercept the Serbian rebels. The latter, however, resorted to guerilla warfare, alternately harrassing the imperial troops and retiring into inaccessible mountainous territory. These rather limited Byzantine operations were interrupted during the winter and Manuel returned to Constantinople, where he staged a triumphal entry signalizing the reconquest of Corfù from the Normans.[16] The island had been taken by the Byzantines in the summer of 1149 and this was supposed to be the first step toward the materialization of Manuel's plan for an invasion of southern Italy in cooperation with Conrad III. The Serb revolt forced Manuel to interrupt his preparations for the invasion, and the festivities arranged at the capital on the occasion of a minor victory were probably intended to obscure the failure of the original plan, the invasion of Italy.

Hostilities between the Byzantine emperor and the Serbs were resumed in the autumn of 1150. This time Cinnamus mentions the presence of Hungarian and Pecheneg auxiliary troops fighting on the side of the rebels. These had been sent by Géza II at Pervoslav's request. Géza himself was at that time engaged in a Russian campaign in support of Isiaslav against George Dolgoruki and Vladimirko.[17]

Manuel's punitive expedition in 1150 was successful. After several minor skirmishes in the region of the river Drina, he forced the Serbs to submit. Pervoslav asked for mercy and was retained in his position as zupan of Rascia, and the earlier ties of vassalage between the Serbs and the empire were renewed.

The Serbian campaign and the close cooperation between Hungary and the Serbian rebels must have convinced

Manuel of the hostile sentiments of the Hungarian court. His main grievance, however, seems to have been Hungary's interference with the affairs of Kiev, a territory which Byzantium considered its own sphere of interest.[18] At any rate, after the submission of the Serbs, Manuel sent a letter to Géza which was equivalent to a declaration of war, enumerating the grievances which the empire had endured and declaring his intention of bringing the war to Hungary.

Manuel launched his first attack against Hungary in the autumn of 1151. At the time Géza II was still fighting against Vladimirko in Halich. Manuel's campaign was a large scale military operation with naval forces also participating. Byzantine warships sailed from Constantinople to the Danube and thence upstream toward Belgrade; the army marched through the valley of the Morava northward to Belgrade which was the point of concentration. Manuel personally conducted the operations. The army, without waiting for the arrival of the ships, crossed the river Sava. While a contingent under the command of Theodore Vatatzes laid siege to Semlin, the town opposite Belgrade, the rest of the army, led by the emperor, penetrated Hungarian territory above the junction of the Danube and Sava rivers. This was the ancient Francochorion, a territory which, together with the town of Sirmium, had been in the possession of Hungary since the time of Andrew I about a century before. The invasion, which took the region by surprise, caused great destruction in the densely populated province. According to Cinnamus, a large part of the population was deported by the Byzantine army and resettled later in some distant underpopulated area of the empire.

Manuel's expedition had a merely punitive character, however, and the Byzantine army did not occupy the Francochorion permanently. After the surrender of Semlin, Manuel ordered a withdrawal. But the Byzantines were

still in Hungarian territory when a Hungarian army, returning from the Russian campaign, arrived on the scene
under the command of Belos. The Hungarians were unable
to cross the Danube and cut off Manuel's retreat because
the Byzantine fleet had finally arrived and controlled the
river. Belos therefore led his army along the northern bank
to a point opposite the Byzantine border stronghold of
Branicevo.[19] Manuel followed this move with his army on
the southern bank and for some time the two armies took
up defensive positions on opposite sides of the river.

At this point Boris appeared on the scene. After the
second crusade, when Louis VII refused his extradition
to Hungary, Boris had returned to Constantinople and
joined Manuel's expedition against Hungary, hoping that
with the aid of the Byzantine army he would be able to
rally a group of Hungarian partisans to assist him in obtaining the throne. Near Branicevo Boris did actually succeed in crossing the Danube with a Byzantine detachment
and penetrated into the valley of the river Temes, deep
in Hungarian territory. On the arrival of superior Hungarian forces, however, he was forced to return to the
southern bank of the Danube. Apart from this isolated
venture, the two armies did not undertake any action against
each other and remained in their positions until Géza arrived
with the rest of the Hungarian army. Probably because his
men were still exhausted from the Russian campaign, the
king did not attack the Byzantines. Instead, he offered to
negotiate.

A peace treaty was, therefore, concluded between Manuel and Géza probably early in 1151, but there is no information available about its conditions. Manuel's Hungarian campaign evidently was presented to the people of
Constantinople as a major victory. Both Cinnamus and
Nicetas give descriptions of his triumphant return to the
capital followed by a long line of Hungarian prisoners,

soldiers and civilians alike. The historians note also some rumors that, since no important enemy commanders had been captured, the emperor ordered several common prisoners to be dressed in fine clothing that made them look like captives of superior rank.[20]

The peace did not last long. In fact, the campaign of 1151 was only the start of a long series of hostilities between the empire and Hungary. From 1151 to 1172, Manuel, in order to check Hungarian interference with Byzantine spheres of interest, conducted ten major campaigns against Hungary. And if he succeeded in keeping Hungary's advance in the Balkans under control, the continuous military preparedness on the Danube frontier tied down important imperial forces which otherwise could have been used very effectively in southern Italy against the Normans. It was largely because of his campaigns in the Balkans that Manuel could not strike with the full force of the empire against Roger II. In fact, the imbroglio in the Balkans and the conflict with Hungary was of decisive significance for Manuel's western political interests. This was to be recognized somewhat belatedly by Manuel when, following the death of Géza II, he began to concentrate his efforts to gain full control of Hungary.

Nevertheless, at the time of the successful conclusion of the Hungarian campaign in 1151, it seemed as if Manuel would be able to devote all his forces to the main goal of his foreign policy, the destruction of Norman power in southern Italy. In September, 1151, after the rupture between Pope Eugenius III and Roger, the Norman kingdom in Italy was isolated. Conrad III, in full understanding with the pope, made final preparations for his Italian campaign, which was to get under way in the fall of the following year and was to be coordinated with a similar move by Manuel against the Normans in southern Italy. It was amidst these favorable expectations that Conrad's death in February, 1152 deprived Manuel of his staunch ally and dealt a heavy blow to his Italian plans.

The accession of Conrad's successor, Frederick I Barbarossa, brought substantial changes in German-Byzantine relations. Frederick's political aspirations, like Manuel's, presupposed considerable control over Italy. Although Frederick found it necessary to adjust his ambitions to the realities of Italian politics, the Norman-Sicilian kingdom formed a serious obstacle to his aims.[21] Frederick clearly recognized the value of the Byzantine alliance against the Normans—the alliance which his father, Conrad, strongly recommended to him on his deathbed—yet he was in no way disposed to share control of Italy with the Byzantine Empire in return for the alliance.

Although Frederick considered himself strong enough to deal with the Normans without the help of Byzantium, it was essential for him to secure the cooperation and approval of the pope. In March, 1153 a new treaty was concluded at Constance between the pope and Barbarossa, replacing the previous agreements between Eugenius III and Conrad. In this treaty Eugenius promised Barbarossa the imperial crown in return for German help in restoring papal authority in Rome against the republican rule of Arnold of Brescia. The pope also consented to Frederick's demand that after the expulsion of the Normans from southern Italy, no Italian territory should be restituted to the Byzantine emperor. Both parties agreed not to conclude separate treaties with the king of Sicily or with the Roman rebels. The treaty did not even recognize Manuel's imperial title, for it referred to him only as *rex* and not as *imperator*.[22]

Frederick also modified his predecessor's Hungarian policy. While Conrad had considered Hungary a Byzantine sphere of interest, Frederick, soon after his accession, decided to compel Hungary to recognize German suzerainty as it had about a century earlier at the time of the Emperor Henry III.[23] For this purpose he was planning a campaign against Hungary as early as 1152, shortly after he ascended the throne. The German feudal nobility, however, at the Diet of Regensburg in July, 1152, rejected Frederick's plan concerning Hungary. According to Otto of Freising, the princes objected to the plan "for certain obscure reasons" and postponed it to "a more opportune time."[24] Perhaps the real obstacle to a German intervention in Hungary in 1152 was the rivalry between Henry the Lion and Henry of Babenberg (Jasomirgott) for possession of Bavaria. The fact that Henry of Babenberg, Frederick's uncle and duke of Austria, was married to Manuel's niece Theodora and did not want to disturb his good relations with Manuel, may also have affected the decision.[25]

Paradoxically, it was then Henry Babenberg's moderation and loyal attitude toward Manuel, perhaps, which saved Hungary in 1152 from a German invasion. Momentarily free from the German danger, Géza II was able to resume hostilities against Byzantium and this contributed to a further delay in Manuel's action against the Normans. In this new campaign against Manuel which started in 1152, Géza hoped to attain the liberation of the Hungarian prisoners captured by the Byzantines in the previous campaign.

Manuel, who was informed in time about the Hungarian preparations, again personally took command of the defenses on the Danube frontier. Géza, seeing that the effect of surprise was lost, did not attempt to cross the Danube and again offered to negotiate. Probably because of the changed situation in Germany, Manuel did not press the issue either. It was agreed that the major part of the Hungarian prisoners would be released and returned to Hungary.[26]

The year 1153 marked a temporary improvement in German-Byzantine relations. The treaty of Constance, a

reaffirmation of the understanding between the pope and
the German emperor which excluded Byzantine interference
from Italy, was only a few months old when one of its
signatories, Pope Eugenius III, died in July, 1153. After
the brief pontificate of Anastasius IV, Hadrian IV ascended
the papal throne in December, 1154.

It seems that Frederick Barbarossa at this time was
inclined to a more friendly attitude toward Byzantium.
He intended to start the long overdue Italian campaign
against the Normans in the fall of 1154 and in view of
the new situation, in the pontificate of Rome, he received
favorably Byzantine overtures to renew the old alliance
which had existed between Manuel and Conrad.

Thus, throughout the year of 1153 intensive negotiations went on between the Byzantine and the German courts.
In his first reply to Manuel's message, Frederick informed
the latter of his decision to march into Italy the following
year and expressed in principle his readiness to renew the
alliance. At the same time he asked the Byzantine emperor
to grant him the hand of an imperial princess.[27]

Contemporary sources concerning the subsequent negotiations between Manuel and Frederick are rather frag-
mentary and incomplete. A passage of Cinnamus, as well
as Manuel's letter to Wibald, abbot of Corvey, former
guardian of Barbarossa and a staunch supporter of the
German-Byzantine alliance, indicates that Manuel favored
Barbarossa's marriage proposal and that his choice fell on
his cousin Princess Maria, the daughter of the sebastocrator
Isaac.[28] Otherwise, from the fact that Manuel's envoys, who
arrived with his answer to Frederick in November, 1153,
almost immediately interrupted the negotiations and returned to Byzantium, one can conclude that Manuel and
Frederick could not agree on the conditions of their common operations against Roger. Evidently Frederick was
less inclined than Conrad had been to tolerate a Byzantine

presence in southern Italy which would interfere with his imperial authority.[29]

Nevertheless, negotiations between the two emperors were repeatedly resumed during the years 1154-1157. In 1158, finally aware of Frederick's pretensions for unchallenged control of Italy and recognizing that the real obstacle to his imperial plans was the German emperor rather than the Norman-Sicilian king, Manuel gave up the idea of the Byzantine-German alliance.

During these years the situation in the Balkans and the attitude of Hungary continued to disturb Manuel's political schemes. Probably around 1153, a new Serb rebellion broke out; an attempt was made to remove the Serbian zupan Pervoslav, who had been previously confirmed in his position by Manuel, and to replace him by his ambitious brother Dessa. This new rebellion prompted Manuel to personally lead an army against the Serbs and to return Pervoslav to power. Pervoslav, however, was compelled to recognize once more the suzerainty of the Byzantine emperor and to renounce the Hungarian alliance.[30]

The other disturbing factor in the Danube-Balkan area remained Hungary. The negotiations between Manuel and Barbarossa and the temporary improvement in Byzantine-German relations created a dangerous situation for Hungary. Géza II was probably informed of Barbarossa's intention of invading Hungary in 1152. Being aware of the growing danger from the expansionist policy of the German emperor, he sought to strengthen the Hungarian-Slavonic alliance by establishing friendly ties with both the Norman-Sicilian kingdom and the West. Cinnamus' suggestion about Norman-Hungarian cooperation seems to be corroborated by a diplomatic document which testifies to the presence of a Hungarian ambassador at the court of Roger II.[31]

Besides establishing contacts with the Sicilian kingdom, Géza's government found allies against Manuel at the

Byzantine court itself, among members of the imperial family. Since Manuel had as yet no male heir, Andronicus Comnenus nurtured secret hopes for the succession. He was the first cousin of Manuel, and son of the Sebastocrator Isaac Comnenus, John II's brother. Andronicus was also an intimate friend of the *basileus*. Manuel, however, showed excessive favors also toward his nephew John Comnenus, whose sister Eudocia was Andronicus' mistress, and John, because of this liaison, felt implacable hatred against his sister's seducer. Andronicus, therefore, became jealous of his young rival and started his intrigues against the emperor. When Manuel appointed him as governor of Niš and Branicevó, the frontier district on the Danube, Andronicus entered into secret negotiations with Géza. He promised the cession of the territory under his control to Hungary, provided Géza helped him to overthrow Manuel and obtain the imperial throne for himself.[32] Cinnamus also informs us of an unsuccessful attempt on the life of the *basileus* instigated by Andronicus.[33] When Andronicus began to give open expression to his hatred of John Comnenus and continued his machinations against Manuel, the emperor ordered his arrest.[34]

In 1155 Géza II, who had previously reached an agreement with Andronicus and did not know about his arrest, invaded Byzantine territory and laid siege to Branicevo. Instead of the expected aid from Andronicus, however, he received word that a large Byzantine force was approaching, led by the emperor himself. Géza raised the siege and began a retreat toward Belgrade, which had been defended by John Cantacuzene. During this retreat a Byzantine detachment which tried to block the way of the Hungarians was defeated and, according to Cinnamus, a Hungarian prince or pretender, possibly Stephen, Géza's brother, was also present in the Byzantine army.[35] Nicetas, on the other hand, speaks about an attack of the Cumans, who, probably in connection with Géza's campaign of 1155 and in his service, invaded Byzantine territory and defeated the troops which were sent against them. According to Nicetas, it was in this battle that the pretender Boris, son of Coloman, met his death.[36]

While both the plot of Andronicus and the Hungarian invasion of 1155 were on the whole unsuccessful, these events had certain repercussions on the affairs of southern Italy. Here the death of Roger II in 1154 created a new political situation. The accession of Roger's son, William I, to the throne of Norman-Sicily did not meet universal approval among the Norman nobility, and William, facing internal opposition and a possible German-Byzantine aggression, offered to negotiate peace with Byzantium.[37] Manuel, who still hoped for an understanding with Frederick Barbarossa, turned down the offer. The negotiations between the German emperor and Manuel, however, remained fruitless, and in October, 1154 Barbarossa started his Italian expedition, which culminated in his coronation as Roman emperor by Pope Hadrian IV in June, 1155. Manuel, concerned about the possibility of an independent German move against the Normans, made a new attempt to induce Barbarossa to join in concerted action. The opposition of his German vassals, however, forced Barbarossa to abandon the idea of an expedition against the Normans. When Manuel's envoys arrived at Ancona, offering him the hand of a Byzantine princess and precious gifts, the emperor had already decided to return to Germany.[38]

Manuel now decided to take independent action against Norman-Sicily. His representatives, Michael Paleologus and John Ducas, began to organize the rebellious elements of the Norman nobility of Apulia, former enemies of Roger II, among them Robert, count of Loritello and cousin of the new king. The rebellion of the discontented

Norman nobility in southern Italy spread rapidly and was
promoted also by false reports of the death of William I,
who was seriously ill during the last months of 1155.
Byzantine troops under the command of Paleologus succeeded in occupying the important port of Bari. Byzantine
diplomats also entered into negotiations with Pope Hadrian IV, who was disappointed by Barbarossa's departure
from Italy and asked the help of the *basileus* against the
king of Sicily.[39]

These promising initial successes, however, were more
the results of Manûel's clever diplomacy and of internal
dissensions among the Normans than of military supe-
riority. The Byzantine commanders, Paleologus and Ducas,
lacking sufficient forces, were unable to exploit the situation and to secure effective control over the territory occupied by the Norman rebels.

The situation was abruptly changed in 1156 by the appearance of large Norman forces. William I, who had
recovered from his illness, reorganized his army and came
to the relief of Brindisi, which was besieged by the Byzantines. In the battle which followed, the major part of the
Byzantine forces in southern Italy, together with their
commanders, Ducas and Bryennius, were captured by the
Normans. Thus the Italian campaign, which started so
promisingly, ended at the end of May, 1156 in a military
disaster for Manuel.[40]

The defeat ruined Manuel's hopes concerning southern
Italy. William suppressed the rebels and in June, 1156
also forced the pope, who was besieged by the Normans
in Benevento, to sign a treaty recognizing the rights of
the kingdom of Sicily over the disputed papal territories
in southern Italy.[41]

In Byzantium, Ducas and Bryennius were held responsible for the military disaster because of their failure to
evacuate the troops from Brindisi in time. The modern

historian is more inclined to put the blame on Manuel himself. He failed to employ sufficient military forces in southern Italy and based his action almost entirely on diplomatic and financial aid supplied to the Norman rebels.[42] In evaluating the causes which led to the disastrous outcome of the Italian campaign of 1155, it must be also remembered that at the time when the campaign started under the command of Paleologus and Ducas, Andronicus' conspiracy and Géza's invasion occupied Manuel's full attention. Evidently the situation on the Danube frontier in 1155 was deemed serious enough to make the emperor's presence there imperative. It was he who personally commanded the defense against the Hungarian invasion, and even after the successful conclusion of the campaign it was necessary to retain strong forces in the Balkans. The military weakness of Byzantium in southern Italy, therefore, was partly a result of the Hungarian aggression and the tense situation which reigned on the Danube frontier and in the Balkans.[43]

Manuel's Italian campaign also marks the beginning of a complete breach between Germany and Byzantium. If Barbarossa in 1154 was still inclined to enter a German-Byzantine alliance against the Normans, after 1155 he realized that the independent action of Byzantium threatened his own claims for control of Italy and abandoned the idea of cooperation. When Manuel's envoys appeared at the German court in June, 1156 and renewed the offer of a Byzantine royal bride, Barbarossa rejected the offer. He had already chosen for his wife Beatrix, the daughter and heiress of Rainald, count of Burgundy, and married her that same month.[44]

The idea of joint action against Hungary, proposed by Manuel for September, 1156 in retaliation for the Hungarian aggression of the previous year, was just as emphatically rejected by Barbarossa.[45] In fact, in the changed political situation, he seemed to recognize the strategic value of Hungary as a buffer state between Germany and the Byzantine Empire. Vladislav, the duke of Bohemia, who had obtained the royal crown from Barbarossa and was related to Géza II, was probably the intermediary in attempts to win Hungary over to the German orbit. The atmosphere for a German-Hungarian rapprochement was the more favorable because after the campaign of 1155 Géza II expected the renewal of hostilities with Manuel.

In fact, in the spring and summer of 1156 Manuel completed preparations for a punitive action against Hungary and the Byzantine fleet had already sailed up the Danube to support the invasion. At this point Géza sent his envoys to the imperial camp to sue for peace and offer the return of the prisoners and booty taken by the Hungarians in the previous campaign. Manuel was anxious to resume operations in Italy. He accepted the offer and abandoned plans for the invasion.[46]

Géza's position had been rendered difficult by the attitude of his younger brother, Stephen, who was claiming the right of succession for himself against Géza's young son, whose name was also Stephen. Like the earlier pretender, Boris, Géza's brother also sought Byzantine support.

For Hungary, therefore, the consequence of the breach between Barbarossa and Manuel was a return to the old policy of balance. At this moment this meant alliance with the German emperor against Byzantium. In fact, even in 1158 a few Hungarian contingents participated in Barbarossa's Italian campaign, serving as auxiliaries in the army of the duke of Austria.[47]

Hungary's dependence on the German Empire, its virtual vassal status, was further emphasized in the last years of Géza's reign by the fact that in the dispute which arose about the succession to the throne both Géza and his brother, the pretender Stephen, requested the arbitration of Frederick Barbarossa. Stephen apparently had not found immediate attention for his cause at Manuel's court and asked the German emperor for support against his brother. Barbarossa, however, did not want to alienate Géza II and invited him to send his envoys to the imperial diet at Regensburg. Here, in 1158, the emperor acted as arbiter in the Hungarian throne dispute. Since Barbarossa left the affair essentially undecided, Géza II remained in a rather insecure position and, therefore, more closely tied to the German alliance. Stephen, on the other hand, left the German court and returned to Constantinople where Manuel, recognizing his value as a new pretender for the Hungarian throne, now received him more favorably. Stephen remained in Constantinople enjoying Manuel's favor. Eventually the emperor gave him his cousin, the daughter of the sebastocrator Isaac, in marriage. This was the princess Maria, who had previously been designated as future bride for Barbarossa.[48] Stephen's presence at the Byzantine court gained real significance after Géza II's death, for Manuel supported his candidacy to the Hungarian throne against Géza's son. At the moment Stephen personified in the eyes of a strong party in Hungary the effort to free the country from the overwhelming influence of Frederick Barbarossa and the reorientation of Hungarian policies toward Byzantium.

The alliance with the German Empire also enabled Géza II to revive Hungary's interests on the Adriatic coast. Avoiding any further conflict with Byzantium, Géza in the last years of his reign led a campaign against Venice and reconquered the important city of Zara which since 1117, the reign of Stephen II, had been in the possession of the Venetian republic.[49]

The close cooperation with Germany was probably responsible also for Hungary's attitude at the beginning of the papal schism which developed after the death of Pope

Hadrian IV in 1159 between Pope Alexander III and Barbarossa's protégé, Victor IV. The king of Hungary had been among the monarchs who were invited by Frederick Barbarossa to send their envoys to the council of Pavia.[50] Géza II first leaned toward the choice of the imperial party, Pope Victor IV, and his representative was present at the council which in February, 1160 excommunicated Alexander III. In the question of the recognition of Victor IV, however, Géza was able to withhold his decision until further consultation with the prelates of Hungary and from 1161 on there was an important change in the relations between Hungary and the papacy.[51]

Alexander III succeeded in rallying behind him the major part of the Christian world. Although in 1162 he was forced to leave Italy temporarily and take refuge in France, the kings of France, England, Sicily, the Spanish kingdoms, most of the Italian cities of Lombardy, and the Latin Christian principalities of the Holy Land recognized him as legitimate head of the Church. Géza II, who had maintained friendly relations with Louis VII, king of France, since the Second Crusade, probably followed the advice of his old friend. At all events, in 1161 he had already notified Louis that he would recognize Pope Alexander III. In this change the Hungarian archbishop of Esztergom, Lucas Bánfi, also played an important role. Important too, was the conciliatory attitude of Alexander III in the question of the appointment of archbishops. He agreed that the Hungarian king would be empowered to confer the *pallium* on the Hungarian archbishops, and also that the king would be intermediary for all communications between members of the Hungarian clergy and the papal court.[52]

The first political consequence of Géza's new ecclesiastical policy was that no Hungarian auxiliaries followed Barbarossa in 1161, when he again entered Italy. The alienation of Hungary from the German Empire is marked also by

Géza's offer to Louis VII for a defensive alliance against Barbarossa. The offer was made in 1161, simultaneously with Géza's letter to Louis concerning the recognition of Pope Alexander III. In the same year a new truce of five years was concluded between Géza and Manuel. This may not have represented a decisive change in Hungary's attitude toward Byzantium, but it certainly brought about a relaxation in the tense and hostile atmosphere which had characterized Byzantine-Hungarian relations during the earlier years of Géza's reign. The rapprochement toward Byzantium also gave Hungary more freedom of action in freeing herself from the pressure of Germany.[53]

The recognition of Alexander III and the truce with Manuel were Géza's last two important political acts. In May, 1162, in his thirty-third year, this unusually gifted ruler and diplomat, one of the most talented members of the Árpád dynasty, died. He was survived by his two young sons, his successor, Stephen III, and the future king, Béla III, as well as by two brothers, both hungry for power, Stephen and Ladislas.

Both the new Hungarian policy toward the Holy See and the new rapprochement with Byzantium were fitting into much vaster political schemes. One was Pope Alexander's conception of a great league of Christian princes against Frederick Barbarossa. This league, which would include the Byzantine emperor as well, would bring about the reunification of western and eastern Christianity under the pope's supremacy and at the same time would counteract Frederick's efforts towards the reassertion of his imperial supremacy over Italy and Rome as a *sacrum imperium*, based on secular foundations and military conquest.[54]

Manuel on the other hand intended to use the league for his own political aims, and in return for the recognition of papal supremacy and the union of the Christian Churches endeavored to secure for himself, with papal support, the imperial throne of Rome. Since Manuel's conception was evidently conflicting with the imperial policy of Barbarossa, Hungary, as a strategic area in the event of a conflict with Germany, was again to play an important role in Manuel's scheme. For this reason, Manuel, after the breach with Barbarossa, concentrated on gaining permanent influence in Hungary, first by force, subsequently by diplomatic means.

CHAPTER V

Hungary in the Byzantine Orbit

THE failure of the campaign in southern Italy in 1156 led to a radical reappraisal of Byzantine foreign policy in the West. To be sure, Manuel's ultimate objective remained, as before, to secure the imperial crown of Rome and, with a possible reunion of the Eastern and Western Churches, to revive the unity of the Christian world under his own authority. Concerning the ways to attain this objective, however, some drastic changes had been made.

The first evidence of a radically new Byzantine foreign policy was the conclusion of a peace treaty with the Norman-Sicilian kingdom, which until then had been considered the greatest obstacle in the way of Byzantine interests in Italy. It was the papal *curia* which mediated the peace in 1158 between Manuel and William I.[1] We can easily presume that it was not the military defeat inflicted by the Normans in 1156 which prompted the *basileus* to this decisive step. After all, the Byzantine forces employed in the Italian campaign were only a fraction of Byzantium's military power, which at the time of the campaign had been divided between Italy and the Balkans. The outcome of the campaign alone would not have discouraged Manuel from pursuing his objectives in Italy or continuing the fight against the Normans. It was rather the experiences of the years 1154-1156 which must have revealed to him that the real threat and the greatest obstacle to his plans concerning the domination of Italy was not the Sicilian kingdom but

the German Empire. By 1157 it was clear that the onetime
alliance with Conrad against Norman-Sicily was definitely
a thing of the past and that Manuel could not count on the
support of a major rival against a minor enemy. Rather
he must seek understanding with all political powers in
Italy—with the pope and the king of Sicily as well as with
the Lombard cities—against the real adversary, Frederick
Barbarossa, whose aim was, if not the *dominium mundi,*
at least the unchallenged control of Italy.

There was also a third participant in the great contest
of power of the twelfth century for exclusive authority in
Christian Europe. Pope Alexander III represented in the
opinion of the majority of the western world the supreme,
exclusive spiritual authority, the *sacerdotium mundi,* which
should be entirely independent from the temporal authority
of the emperor. In the conflict between Alexander and
Barbarossa, many of the leading intellects of the western
world, like John of Salisbury, raised their voice in defense
of papal independence and freedom of the Church, protest-
ing against the procedure followed at the Council of Pavia
in 1160, and arguing that the head of the Christianity
should not be submitted to any single nation, since his authority is universal.[2]

In his conflict with Frederick Barbarossa and the anti-
pope Victor IV, Alexander III was forced to leave Italy.
At Montpellier, where he sought asylum from Barbarossa
in 1162, Alexander attempted to form a diplomatic combination which would be composed of France, Norman
Sicily, and the Byzantine Empire. This was a rather bold
and ambitious program since two of these powers, Sicily
and Byzantium, themselves represented, through their presence or ambitions in the Italian peninsula, a threat to the
Patrimonium Petri. Furthermore, these two powers had
conflicting interests.[3] Nevertheless, the change in Byzantine

foreign policy and the peace treaty of 1158 between Manuel and William I served well the interests of the papacy.

Apparently papal diplomacy had also been active in eastern Europe. Along with the recognition of Alexander by Géza II, papal mediation facilitated the truce between Manuel and Géza in 1161. Burchard, Barbarossa's imperial notary, accuses Alexander III of conspiring with Manuel against the German emperor and of promising him the *"vanitatum vanitas,"* i.e., the imperial crown and the transfer of the seat of the Roman Empire from Rome to Constantinople.[4] Again it is Burchard who describes the meeting in 1161 of the representatives of five rulers to discuss plans for concerted action against Barbarossa.[5] Since Burchard belonged to the supporters of the anti-pope Victor IV, his statements about Alexander III may well be prejudiced. It is, nevertheless, true that Alexander, after his election to the papal throne, had been trying to form a great alliance against Barbarossa which would include the Byzantine emperor as well.

In 1161 Alexander sent Cardinal William of Pavia as his legate to the Byzantine court to solicit recognition of his claim to the papacy by the *basileus.* Negotiations between the pope and Manuel continued through the years 1163-65. At the same time, Louis VII, probably at the request of Alexander, also tried to persuade Manuel to recognize the election of Alexander III. Thus in 1163 secret negotiations were going on in France between the envoys of Louis VII, Manuel, and the pope. During these negotiations William of Pavia, the papal legate, went as far as declaring that the imperial title of Rome had long been usurped by barbarians. This was obviously a reference to the Germans and it seemed to indicate that according to the papal view, Manuel was regarded as lawful heir of the Roman emperors and not Barbarossa.

It would seem that Manuel and Alexander were not far from reaching an agreement. In fact, in 1166 Manuel made a formal offer to end the schism of the churches and to recognize Pope Alexander III as head of the Roman Church, "sacrosanct mother of all churches." But when he asked the pope in turn to send him the imperial crown of Rome, Alexander's answer was evasive. The pope referred to the problem as one which exceeded his jurisdiction and had to be deliberated with his cardinals.[6]

The negotiations between Alexander III and Manuel ultimately ended in a deadlock. The matter which separated Manuel and the pope during the negotiations was that of the capital of the empire. The pope asked that the seat of the imperial government be transferred to Rome, the historical capital of the empire, while Manuel wanted to retain the center of the empire at Constantinople.[7]

Although the negotiations did not lead to the results desired by Manuel, he continued to support Alexander's project of a coalition against Frederick Barbarossa, for this corresponded with his own political aims in the West.[8] His ultimate goal was, as indicated before, the imperial authority of Rome, and this presupposed control of Italy. For the time being this goal seemed to be attainable through cooperation with the papacy and, to a lesser degree, with the Norman-Sicilian king against the major rival, the German emperor. This conception was reflected, as has been indicated, by the peace treaty between Manuel and William I.

But there was still another important area of contact between Byzantium and its German rival: the Danube basin and the Balkans. After 1156 there were no further hostilities on the Danube frontier; nevertheless, the situation there remained tense, especially after the definite estrangement between Byzantium and Germany and the temporary alignment of Hungary with Frederick Barbarossa between 1156 and 1160 (p. 84).

The new rapprochement between Géza II and Manuel shortly before Géza's death, therefore, not only served the purpose of easing the tension, but also of drawing Hungary away from the German orbit into the Byzantine sphere of influence. It might also transform this important buffer-state into a bulwark of Byzantine expansion towards the West. The death of Géza II. in May, 1162 provided a favorable opportunity for Manuel to intervene directly in Hungarian affairs and to secure the succession for a protégé who would follow his lead in foreign policy.

In Hungary, as in Kievan Russia, the succession to the throne did not necessarily follow the rule of primogeniture, for ancient custom recognized the rights of the dead king's eldest brother. Strong-minded rulers like Coloman or Géza II tried to secure the throne during their lifetime for their sons. This practice frequently led to enmity or even to an open breach between the king and his brothers. Often they were forced to flee the country in order to escape imprisonment or mutilation, as had been the fate of Almos, who was blinded at the behest of his brother Coloman. To make things worse, the dynasty of the Arpáds seems to have been afflicted by early deaths of the ruling monarchs. The medieval kings of Hungary usually died in their thirties, leaving —if they had sons—a child on the throne. This situation very often led to a conflict between the king's party and the party of a pretender, usually an uncle of the young king.[9]

This was precisely the situation which arose in Hungary after the death of Géza II. His son, Stephen III, was fifteen years old when he succeeded his father. In the face of a fairly strong opposition which advocated a return to the old custom of succession, the young king's party, led by the dowager queen, Euphrosyne, Archbishop Lucas Bánfi, and the *comes palatinus,* Denis, hastily proceeded with the coronation.[10]

As was indicated before, Géza's youngest brother Stephen had already announced his claims to the Hungarian throne in 1158 while Géza was still alive. After failing to obtain a favorable decision from Barbarossa at the Regensburg arbitration in 1158, he went from Germany to Constantinople. Here he was given a friendly reception by Manuel and was married to the emperor's cousin, Princess Maria. Stephen was followed very soon by his older brother Ladislas, who had also been forced to leave Hungary by a conflict with the king. Encouraged by Stephen's success, Ladislas went to Constantinople, was granted asylum, and enjoyed the emperor's hospitality. He was also offered a marriage in the imperial family, but, with some diplomatic foresight, declined the offer. Apparently he was anxious to avoid the appearance of depending entirely on the Byzantine emperor.

Upon receiving news of Géza's death and Stephen III's accession, Manuel and the Hungarian pretenders immediately went into action. Manuel saw a favorable opportunity to build up Byzantine influence in Hungary by putting one of his protégés on the throne. He was then at the apex of his power. He was at peace with Norman-Sicily and engaged in promising negotiations with the papacy which opened new prospects toward widening his prestige and influence in the western world. In addition, he had recently obtained, around the end of 1161, the submission of Kilidj Arslan, the sultan of Iconium, in a treaty which gave Byzantium a respite in the East and consequently more freedom of action in the West. Furthermore, following the death of the Empress Bertha-Irene in 1160, Manuel's marriage to Marie of Antioch, daughter of Raimond of Poitiers and Constance, princess of Antioch, which was concluded on December 25, 1161, secured for Byzantium the control of Antioch against the interference of Baldwin III, king of Jerusalem.[11]

Manuel first supported Stephen's candidacy to the Hungarian throne. Accordingly, in the spring of 1162, Stephen appeared with a Byzantine escort on the Hungarian border at Belgrade. Apparently there existed a strong party in Hungary which was in favor of preserving the old rule of succession and was ready to offer the crown to one of the brothers of the deceased king. This can be concluded also from the fact that the dowager queen together with the young king, Stephen, and their followers found it advisable to transfer their residence hastily to the western frontier and install themselves in the fortress of Pozsony (Pressburg).[12] Meanwhile, Manuel also left Constantinople and established his headquarters in the Balkans—in Sophia or in Philippopolis—in order to follow closely the negotiations between the Byzantine ambassadors and the leaders of the Hungarian rebel party.[13] It soon turned out that the Hungarians were reluctant to accept the pretender Stephen for their king, mainly because they feared that Stephen, through his relations to the imperial family, would transform Hungary into a vassal state of Byzantium. Another, rather formal objection was that among the surviving brothers of the late king, Stephen was the younger, whereas according to the old custom, the crown should go to the elder brother, Ladislas, who conveniently happened to¹ be entirely free from family ties with the emperor.[14]

Facing this opposition, Manuel, whose objective was only to place one of his protégés on the Hungarian throne, did not insist on Stephen's candidacy and accepted the Hungarian proposal offering the throne to Ladislas. It was stipulated, however, that after the death of Ladislas the crown would go to Stephen. Ladislas II was crowned by one archbishop of southern Hungary, since the senior archbishop and head of the Church in Hungary, Lucas

Bánfi, refused to officiate at the coronation. The archbishop, a staunch supporter of Pope Alexander III, opposed the Greek orientation of Hungary because he feared the spread of the Orthodox faith at the expense of Latin Christianity.

The reign of Ladislas II lasted barely six months. He died in January, 1163, and according to the agreement with Manuel, his younger brother, Stephen, made another attempt to occupy the throne.[15] This attempt was no more successful than the first. Although he was crowned by the same archbishop who officiated at the coronation of Ladislas II, Stephen IV was unable to maintain himself on the throne against a growing anti-Byzantine opposition led by the powerful Archbishop Lucas. This situation was utilized by partisans of the young Stephen III. They were joined also by the old Ban Belos, who twenty years before during the minority of Géza II, had been virtual regent of Hungary.

The young Stephen's party even secured the support of the German emperor, who saw in the rivalry an opportunity to curb Manuel's influence in Hungary. In 1163 Frederick Barbarossa received a delegation of Hungarian noblemen, partisans of Stephen III, asking his support and offering him a considerable amount of money as a gift. Barbarossa ordered Vladislav, the king of Bohemia, as well as Henry Jasomirgott, the duke of Austria, to give military assistance to Stephen III.[16] Reinforced with this aid and supported by Archbishop Lucas and the majority of the population, Stephen III made a triumphant return. His forces met and defeated the army of Stephen IV in June, 1163. The pretender was captured and brought before his nephew, but Stephen III released him on the advice of Archbishop Lucas. Stephen IV then sought refuge at Manuel's camp in Sophia.[17]

Manuel first seemed to be determined to throw his entire support behind Stephen IV and sent him, with a Byzantine

army under the command of Alexius Kontostephanos, to
the Hungarian border. He himself went to Nis where he
expected the Serbian auxiliaries of the grand zupan Dessa,
later better known as Stephen Nemanja, who had replaced
his brother Pervoslav on the throne of Rascia.[18] Dessa
was Belos' brother and therefore also related to the family
of Géza·II. He showed little enthusiasm for joining the
emperor's expedition against Hungary and sent his contingent to the Byzantine camp only when Manuel threatened
him with reprisals.[19]

After having secured the cooperation of Nemanja,
Manuel proceeded with his troops to the Hungarian border,
but was evidently convinced of his protégé's growing un-
popularity and the uselessness of a military intervention
in his support by information that reached him at Belgrade.
Manuel, therefore, decided to abandon his original plan,
the candidacy of Stephen IV, and to seek a rapprochement
with the existing regime in Hungary. Accordingly, in the
fall of 1163 he sent his personal envoy, George Paleologus,
to Stephen III's court, offering him peace and recognition
as king of Hungary. At the same time Manuel asked
Stephen to send his younger brother, the thirteen-year-old
Prince Béla, to the Byzantine court, where his education
would be completed and he would be engaged to Manuel's
daughter from his first marriage, ten-year-old Princess
Maria.[20]

Although not explicitly mentioned during the negotiations with Stephen III, Manuel's offer had certain impli-
cations which reveal the wider, far-reaching scope of
Manuel's policy with regard to Hungary. It was now the
emperor's purpose not merely to establish family ties between Byzantium and Hungary and to receive a Hungarian
prince at his court in Constantinople, who at the opportune
time might be used as instrument of Byzantine influence in
Hungary. Rather, a more remote but more ambitious

scheme of extending the actual authority of Byzantium over Hungary, of drawing her definitely into the Byzantine orbit by making her a vassal-state and actually part of the empire, seems to have been in the emperor's mind. Such a policy was similar to that earlier pursued with the Balkan nations, the Bulgarians or the Serbians.

Moreover, Manuel had no male heir. Through his marriage with Maria Prince Béla would become a member of the imperial family and a potential successor to the Byzantine throne, and this was an added factor in the emperor's planning. As the Hungarian king's oldest brother, Béla, according to the old custom of succession, was closest in the line to the Hungarian throne. In the event of Stephen III's death, therefore, Béla could even unite the crown of Byzantium with the crown of St. Stephen and thus secure for the Comnenian dynasty and the Byzantine Empire permanent influence and a predominant position in the Danube basin.[21]

These prospects fitted perfectly into Manuel's wider schemes concerning the restoration of a universal empire under Byzantine rule. A personal union between the Byzantine Empire and the Hungarian kingdom would not only put an end to Serb independence movements supported by Hungary, but would give Byzantium a commanding position in eastern central Europe. The control of Hungary in the center of the Danube basin could form the pivot of Byzantine power on the eastern borders of the German empire, ending all German influence there. Further, the possibility of building a similar stronghold for Byzantium in the center of the Mediterranean basin, by gaining control of Italy in cooperation with the papacy, was still open.[22]

The assumption that Manuel's attitude in the feud of the Hungarian princes was motivated by the forementioned prospects, seems to be confirmed by his actions following the agreement with Stephen III. A closer political tie between Byzantium and Hungary through Béla's prospective marriage probably appeared a remote possibility to Stephen and his advisers. But the immediate advantages of Byzantine recognition and the elimination of Stephen IV from the contest were stronger motives, and the Byzantine offer was accepted. In the fall of 1163, the Byzantine delegation accompanied Prince Béla to Constantinople, where he changed his name to Alexius, was converted to the Orthodox faith, and was elevated to the dignity of a *despotes*.[23] This was followed two years later by the official engagement of Béla-Alexius and Manuel's daughter, Maria. In a solemn ceremony in the church of the palace of Blachernes both were proclaimed heirs of the Byzantine throne, while members of the imperial family and the government took an oath of allegiance to them.

There was considerable opposition at the court against the prospective succession of Béla to the Byzantine throne. This opposition was headed by the emperor's cousin, Andronicus, who not long before had been permitted to return from his exile in Russia and who alone in the imperial family refused to take the oath of allegiance to the young Hungarian prince.[24]

Notwithstanding, there is little doubt that Manuel at that time considered Béla his presumptive heir and the most suitable person to realize the unification of Hungary with the Byzantine Empire. The *basileus* himself introduced the young prince to the complex and intricate machinery of Byzantine court, diplomacy, and military affairs, as did the highest dignitaries of the imperial army and civil administration. His education was completed, his mind and manners polished, under the direction of the best Byzantine-Greek and western Latin-French tutors, in the refined atmosphere of the court of Manuel. Béla-Alexius' name is mentioned in second place, immediately after the emperor's, among the dignitaries who were present on May 6, 1166 at the final session of the Council of Constantinople.[25] Even the campaigns which Manuel had to conduct in the years 1164-1167 against Stephen III were conducted in the name of the Despotes Béla-Alexius, in order to protect his interests.[26]

The new conflict with Stephen III broke out very soon after Béla left Hungary for Constantinople, and it arose over the interpretation of the territorial stipulations of the agreement between Manuel and Stephen III. Since the time of Ladislas I, who appointed Almos as viceroy or governor of Croatia, it was customary for the kings of Hungary to assign one part of the kingdom, usually Croatia, to one of their younger sons who had no prospect of succeeding to the throne. These younger princes exerted their authority on the territory assigned to them in the name of the king. Apparently Géza II had assigned Dalmatia and part of Croatia, the territory of the district of Sirmium (the old "Francochorion"), as an appanage to his younger son, Béla, while Stephen, the eldest son, was presumptive heir to the throne.[27]

According to the agreement concluded between Manuel and Stephen III, Prince Béla would retain his appanage even after his departure to the Byzantine court. This practically meant that these territories long-disputed between Byzantium and Hungary would be returned to Byzantine control by the Hungarian king.[28]

The sources are rather obscure and incomplete about the events which followed Béla's departure. It is possible that Stephen III or his advisers changed their minds and failed to transfer the territories in question to the Byzantines. It seems more probable, however, that Béla's uncle, the unsuccessful candidate, Stephen IV, made another attempt without Byzantine aid to reenter Hungary from the Balkans. As a consequence, the government of Stephen III, to prevent Béla's appanage from falling into the pretender's possession, either failed to evacuate these territories or reoccupied them.[29] Whatever the cause of the new conflict, Manuel again mobilized his forces in order to secure the area. He penetrated the southern part of Hungary with a strong army, establishing his headquarters first at Titel, then at Petrikon on the Danube. From there Manuel sent an ultimatum to Stephen demanding the restitution of Dalmatia and Sirmium to Béla.[30]

Manuel's intervention caused considerable consternation in Hungary. Stephen III fled with his court to the western frontier and sought foreign allies against Byzantium. Yaroslav, the prince of Halich, and Vladislav, the king of Bohemia, sent troops in response to a call by the dowager queen. (Yaroslav was son of Vladimirko, the onetime adversary of Géza II, who after the end of the disputes of the Kievan princes over the succession, had restored peaceful relations with Hungary and arranged the engagement of his daughter to Stephen III.[31] Vladislav had already served as intermediary in the rapprochement between Géza II and Barbarossa, and in 1163 had helped Stephen III to defeat his uncle and maintain himself on the Hungarian throne. Géza II before his death recommended his son to the goodwill and protection of Vladislav, whose son, Svyatopolk, was supposed to marry Géza II's daughter.[32])

It was probably the presence of Vladislav in the combined Hungarian-Russian-Czech camp which prevented the armed clash with Manuel. During the Second Crusade Vladislav had served in the army of Conrad III and visited Constantinople, where he had enjoyed Manuel's hospitality and friendship and sworn him personal allegiance. When Manuel was informed of Vladislav's presence in the enemy camp, he sent an envoy to remind him of his oath.[33] The negotiations which followed ended in a complete agreement between the two regarding the position of Stephen III. In a new treaty Manuel reaffirmed his recognition of Stephen on the Hungarian throne, while Stephen promised to restore Béla's appanage, the district of Sirmium an'd Dalmatia. Vladislav, on his part, reaffirmed his friendship with Manuel by sending his granddaughter to Constantinople where she was supposed to marry a member of the imperial family.[34]

Shortly after this treaty a special embassy from Stephen III asked Manuel to prevent the pretender, Stephen IV, from reentering Hungary and to withdraw all support from him.[35] In spite of assurances from the Byzantine government Stephen IV, shortly after Manuel's return to Constantinople, made a new attempt to enter Hungary from Sirmium, which had been evacuated by the Hungarians and was now under Byzantine occupation. He was accompanied only by a group of his own partisans, and without Byzantine support had no prospect of success. After being defeated in Hungarian territory, Stephen retreated to Sirmium. Stephen III's army, however, continued operations against the pretender and in 1165 overran the Byzantine garrison of Sirmium and occupied this strategically important town.[36] Upon hearing this news Manuel sent a personal message to Stephen III accusing him of a breach of the previous agreement.[37]

Byzantine diplomacy had, in fact, already been active in isolating Hungary. Following the mediation of the king of Bohemia in the last conflict with Stephen III, its first objective had been to deprive Hungary of foreign support in any new conflict. This was the purpose of a Byzantine mission sent in 1164 to Ratislav, the prince of Kiev, who was related to Stephen III through his mother, Euphrosyne, daughter of Mstislav, the late prince of Kiev. After settling a' dispute over the nomination of the metropolitan of Kiev, the Byzantine envoys succeeded in inducing Ratislav to conclude a treaty of friendship with Byzantium.[38]

A similar diplomatic gesture was undertaken toward

Yaroslav, the prince of Halich who had given asylum to Manuel's fugitive cousin Andronicus, and by this made himself disliked in Byzantium. Manuel forgave his rebellious cousin and gave him permission to return to Constantinople. Through this step the cause of the friction between Yaroslav and the Byzantine court was eliminated.[39]

Vladislav, the king of Bohemia, had already renewed friendly relations with Byzantium and apparently was ready to abandon the cause of the Hungarian king.[40] Another Byzantine embassy around the same time obtained a promise from the republic of Venice to provide a hundred ships, presumably for an action against the Hungarians in Dalmatia.[41]

After this diplomatic preparation Manuel sent a Byzantine contingent to the aid of Stephen IV, who was besieged by the army of Stephen III in the fortress of Semlin (Zemun) on the Hungarian-Byzantine border. The relieving force, however, was repelled, and Stephen IV died from poison on April 13, 1165. Byzantine sources attribute his death to the work of an agent of Stephen III, a certain Thomas.[42] After the death of Stephen IV the garrison of the town surrendered under terms that permitted the retirement of the defenders to Byzantine territory.

Manuel did not accept this defeat and appeared at the head of an army before Semlin. Stephen III hastily retreated, but left the town occupied by a strong Hungarian detachment. The Byzantines laid siege to the town, but the main force, with the *basileus* in command, prepared for a frontal attack on Stephen's army. Before this encounter could take place, Semlin surrendered after repeated Byzantine attacks. On the intervention of Prince Béla, who was with him in the Byzantine camp, Manuel spared the lives of the defenders.[43] After the fall of Semlin Stephen III proposed peace and agreed to recognize Béla's right to Dalmatia and the territory of Sirmium. Since, according to

Cinnamus, the Byzantine army operating under the command of John Ducas already occupied seventy-five towns in Dalmatia, the offer apparently sanctioned only a *fait accompli*; nevertheless Manuel accepted it and peace was restored.[44]

It was probably after this campaign that Manuel officially proclaimed Prince Béla as his presumptive heir and exacted an oath of allegiance to him from members of his court. This can be concluded from the fact that Andronicus, who until 1165 had been in exile, was already present in Constantinople and refused to participate in the oath taking ceremony.[45]

In the following year the Hungarians made a new attempt to recover the province of Sirmium and invaded the territory held by the Byzantines. During this brief campaign the Hungarian troops inflicted a serious defeat on the forces of the Byzantine governor, Michael Gabras.[46] This new violation of the treaty prompted Manuel to a punitive action against Hungary. This time he sent his future son-in-law Béla with an army to the Hungarian border on the Danube, while other Byzantine forces invaded Hungary from the east and ravaged the unprotected provinces of Transylvania. This Byzantine success, however, was counterbalanced by losses in Dalmatia. A strong Hungarian army invaded the province and defeated the Byzantine garrisons. Even the provincial governor was captured by the Hungarians and the relatively easy reconquest of Dalmatia seems to indicate that the Dalmatian cities sided with the Hungarians.[47]

Meanwhile, there are indications that the diplomatic isolation of Hungary was not complete and that in the years 1166-1167 a temporary rapprochement developed between Hungary and the Venetian republic.[48] Moreover, after the loss of her Russian and Czech allies, Hungary apparently sought the aid or mediation of the German emperor in the conflict. This can be concluded from the fact that in 1166, shortly after the outbreak of the new conflict between Byzantium and Hungary, Henry Jasomirgott, duke of Austria, and Otto of Wittelsbach appeared at Manuel's headquarters in Sophia as Barbarossa's personal envoys and offered to mediate a peaceful solution to the conflict.[49] The mission proved unsuccessful. Manuel was only willing to accord a temporary armistice, but Henry of Austria, on his return from Constantinople, interrupted his journey in Hungary in order to visit Stephen III. On this occasion Stephen, who had earlier dissolved his engagement to Yaroslav's daughter, asked and obtained the hand of Henry's daughter Agnes, and this prospective marriage seemed to secure for Hungary the duke of Austria's future support.[50] In the spring of 1167 Manuel received another Hungarian peace offer at Philippopolis, but no accord was attained.[51]

The plan for a new campaign against Hungary was worked out by Manuel himself, but injuries which he suffered at a tournament prevented him from personally leading his troops. His nephew Andronicus Kontostephanos was, therefore, put in command of the army.[52] During the early summer of 1167 the army arrived without incident at the Hungarian border and again took up its position at Semlin, where Kontostephanos expected the arrival of the enemy. The Hungarian army, under the command of the Comes palatinus, Denis, and reinforced with auxiliary troops of the duke of Austria, arrived on the scene in early July.

According to Nicetas, Manuel at the last moment sent a message to Kontostephanos ordering him to postpone the battle because of some unfavorable astrological predictions. Kontostephanos, however, disregarded the message and gave the order to attack.[53]

There is no information about the strength of the Byzantine army, but apparently the Byzantine commander had detailed reports concerning the enemy's strength. According to Nicetas, the Hungarian army was about fifteen thousand strong, composed partly of heavy armored cavalry and partly of infantry, archers, and light cavalry. The commander of the army was the same Denis who in the previous year had defeated the Byzantine governor, Gabras. Nicetas mentions thirty-seven *ispans* (zupans or company commanders) under Denis' command and also gives some idea of the Hungarian tactics.

Apparently the Hungarian general applied methods of warfare which were customary in the armies of the Lombard cities. His whole army formed a compact body, at its center a banner on a huge mast mounted on a heavy carriage (*carrocium*) drawn by four oxen. Men and horses were protected by heavy iron armor, and from a distance the army looked like a compressed dark mass, drawing its strength from this solid unity.[54]

The Byzantine army was less compactly organized, for it was composed of many heterogeneous elements—Pecheneg and Cuman light cavalry, Byzantine infantry and heavy cavalry, Norman mercenaries, Serbian lancers, Turkish auxiliaries—but this gave it greater flexibility and mobility. Accordingly, the Byzantine commander concentrated his efforts on breaking up the solid line of the Hungarian army.[55]

The two armies met on St. Procopius' Day, July 8, 1167, near Semlin, on the northern bank of the river Sava. The fighting was ferocious and ended with a Byzantine victory. The Hungarian phalanx broke. The commander, Denis, managed to escape, but five zupans, eight hundred men, and the banner were captured by the Byzantines, who also collected some two thousand pieces of armor from the bodies left on the battlefield. The next day they pillaged the abandoned Hungarian camp.[56]

The victory of 1167, which Manuel celebrated with a great triumphal entry into Constantinople, ended his cam-

paigns against Hungary. The Byzantine army did not continue the pursuit of the defeated Hungarian army, but returned with the captives and booty to Constantinople. The
sources are silent about a peace treaty between Manuel and
Stephen III, but apparently the Hungarian king accepted
the loss of Dalmatia and Sirmium as a consequence of the
defeat. At any rate, during his reign there was no further
attempt to recover Béla's appanage.

The Byzantine sources which are so eloquent in describ-
ing Kontostephanos' campaign and victory, do not mention how the Byzantines recovered Dalmatia, which during
the previous year, 1166, had apparently been conquered by
the Hungarians. Whether Dalmatia was evacuated by Hungary and returned to Byzantium as result of a new treaty,
or whether the Byzantine army reconquered it during the
war of 1167, is not known. It seems quite certain, however,
that after the victorious campaign of 1167 Dalmatia and
the district of Sirmium remained in the possession of the
Byzantine Empire for the rest of Manuel's reign.[57] In
fact, this was perhaps the only positive result of Manuel's
repeated campaigns against Stephen III.

Otherwise, Byzantine influence in Hungary, one main
objective of Manuel's diplomacy, seems to have been in
decline, at least during the reign of Stephen III. While
Manuel succeeded in reducing Hungarian-Slav cooperation
in the Balkans, as well as in Halich and Bohemia, he forced
Stephen to seek German support. And the marriage of
Stephen to the daughter of Henry Jasomirgott again
brought Hungary, at least for the lifetime of Stephen III,
into Barbarossa's orbit.

Thus Manuel's last campaign against Stephen III, in
spite of his brilliant military victory, was only a half success. Stephen was able at the cost of considerable territorial
losses to preserve the independence of Hungary. Moreover,
the reconquest of Dalmatia by the Byzantines aroused Vene-

tian concern. Indeed, after 1168 there was a growing tension between the empire and Venice which in 1171 led to an open conflict.

But Manuel's position in the West in the 1160's was still strong. He was negotiating with the pope for the reunion of the Churches. He supported the anti-German Lombard League and in 1166 gave material aid to Milan. He saw in his cooperation with Alexander III and the Sicilian kingdom an important element of his great design for the restoration of the Roman Empire in the West.

In this scheme Hungary continued to play a role of primary importance, although an unforeseen event prompted Manuel to change his earlier plan concerning the succession of the Hungarian Prince Béla in Byzantium and the eventual union of Hungary with the Byzantine Empire. In September, 1169 a son was born to the Empress Maria, Manuel's second wife. With the birth of this son the position of Prince Béla as presumptive heir of the throne was necessarily affected. Manuel had to alter his original decision and proclaimed his newly born son, Alexius, his heir and successor. Béla had to give up also the rank of *despot* and receive the lesser title of *caesar*. With this title he was still, however, regarded as member of the imperial family.[58] At the same time Manuel decided to dissolve Béla's engagement to Maria, who was to play an important part in several other political marriage plans in the near future.[59]

Although the prospects of a personal union between the empire and Hungary vanished with the change in the Byzantine succession, Manuel did not give up his determination to secure some control over Hungary by making the country a Byzantine vassal state. The former heir, Prince Béla, was not at all disgraced. On the contrary, Manuel's attitude toward him indicates that it was his firm intention to keep the presumptive heir to the Hungarian throne in the imperial family of Byzantium.

Shortly after the dissolution of Béla's engagement to Maria, Manuel arranged the marriage of Béla to Anne of Châtillon, stepsister of the Empress Maria and younger daughter of Constance of Antioch.[60] Thus Béla, instead of being the emperor's future son-in-law, became his brother-in-law. Apparently Béla had not resented the changes in his position at the Byzantine court and was patiently awaiting the time when he would occupy the throne of Hungary with the support of Byzantium. Manuel on his part was waiting for the same opportunity, which would enable him to tighten his grip on Hungary. Thus there was no conflict of interest between the *basileus* and his brother-in-law.

The opportunity arrived soon. In 1172 Manuel proclaimed his three-year-old son co-emperor. A few months later, in March, 1172, Stephen III died in his twenty-fourth year, leaving no male heir. In Hungary rumors were circulating which attributed the king's death to poisoning and accused Prince Béla and Manuel of conspiring against Stephen's life.[61] The majority of the country, however, seemed to rally behind Béla's candidacy. When the news of Stephen's death reached Constantinople, Manuel went to Sophia and it was here that he met a Hungarian embassy which had come to offer the crown to Béla. Since there was still considerable opposition against him in Hungary, a strong Byzantine escort under the command of the *protosebastus* John accompanied Béla and his wife to Hungary. Before his departure from Constantinople, Manuel demanded an oath of allegiance from Béla, who promised solemnly to promote "the interests of the emperor and of the Romans." [62]

Opposition against Béla in Hungary was led by Archbishop Lucas, who mistrusted him because of his conversion to the Orthodox faith and refused to officiate at the coronation. Apparently Béla's mother Euphrosyne, who would have preferred her youngest son Géza on the throne, organized resistance against him. Béla, presumably with Byzantine help, acted with firmness. Against the opposition of Archbishop Lucas, he turned directly to the papacy, declaring his allegiance to the Catholic faith and asking the pope to sanction his coronation. Alexander III complied with the request and directed the archbishop of Kalocsa to officiate at the ceremony of coronation.[63] Accordingly, Béla III was crowned king of Hungary early in 1173 and to prove his good intentions toward the Catholic Church, sought reconciliation with the powerful Archbishop Lucas, reaffirming his rights in regard to the coronation of Hungarian kings.

After the coronation, Béla's mother and younger brother fled the country and sought asylum in the court of Henry of Austria; later, the fugitives fled to Bohemian territory. Here Sobieslav II, at the request of Béla III, arrested the dowager queen and her son and extradited them to Hungary. With this the last opposition against Béla's reign collapsed. Béla put his brother into prison and sent his mother to a Byzantine monastery.[64]

With Béla III firmly on the Hungarian throne, Hungary slipped out of Barbarossa's orbit, where she had been pushed temporarily during Stephen III's lifetime by the wars with Manuel. As long as Manuel lived, Béla remained his faithful vassal, maintaining political and cultural relations with Byzantium and France.[65] During Manuel's lifetime he did not even reclaim the possession of his appanage, Dalmatia and Sirmium. When Manuel conducted his expedition in 1176 against Kilidj Arslan, the sultan of Iconium, there were Hungarian auxiliaries under the command of the ban of Croatia and the duke of Transylvania in the Byzantine army. A diploma of a later Hungarian king, Béla IV, granted landed property to the descendants of those Hungarian warriors who fought against the Turks under Ban Ompudin and Duke Leustachius in the Byzantine army.[66]

It can be stated with considerable justification that Manuel's power policies regarding central and western Europe nowhere else found such success than in Hungary and the Balkans. The Serb independence movement was at least temporarily suppressed and Stephen Nemanja forced into submission. The theme of Dalmatia and the district and ancient imperial seat of Sirmium returned to the empire, and the Danube frontier now included the Francochorion, a considerable part of the old imperial province of Pannonia inferior. And beyond this frontier, Hungary, the central power in the Carpathian-Danube basin, was tied to the Byzantine Empire throughout Manuel's lifetime, and even later, until the death of Béla III, first by the bonds of vassalage and later by a free community of interests.

Western Policies and Hungarian Relations During the Last Decade of Manuel's Reign

IF Manuel's Balkan policies were successful insofar as he succeeded in making Hungary a Byzantine satellite, in establishing a strong Byzantine position in the Balkans and the central Danube valley, and in checking there the influence of the Hohenstaufen Empire, his political moves in the Mediterranean area were proceeding less promisingly.

After the failure of his campaign in southern Italy and the peace treaty of 1158 with William I, Manuel's efforts in the West were restricted to diplomatic activities. In the case of Hungary only one country had to be won over, and that by force; in Italy there were several powers which Byzantine diplomacy had to consider in its efforts to challenge Barbarossa's control of northern Italy. These were the papacy, the Sicilian kingdom, the Lombard cities, of which Milan was the most powerful, and the republic of Venice.

As was already indicated, Pope Alexander III, after his breach with Barbarossa, conceived the idea of forming a coalition against the Hohenstaufen emperor which would include the Byzantine Empire. Manuel wholeheartedly supported the plan in the belief that it would help him to secure control of Italy, the most important stronghold in the contest with Barbarossa for the imperial crown of Rome. It seems, however, that the obstacles which stood in the way of the plan were too numerous. The king of Sicily apparently was not enthusiastic about an alliance which would have enabled his powerful former enemy to intervene on Italian soil.[1] Negotiations between Louis VII and Manuel's envoys during 1163-1164 did not have positive results either, and Alexander III had to abandon his cherished idea, a coalition of anti-Hohenstaufen states in Europe.[2]

Nevertheless, contacts between Rome and Constantinople remained friendly. Alexander III's non-committal yet friendly disposition towards Manuel was illustrated in 1171 by his mediation between Louis VII and Manuel concerning a marriage between Louis' daughter Agnes and Manuel's son Alexius, presumptive heir to the throne.[3]

While contacts between Manuel and Alexander III remained constantly cordial, or at least correct, the Italian policy of Byzantium with regard to Sicily and the Venetian Republic was inconsequential and contradictory. After the death of William I in May, 1166, Manuel endeavored to improve relations with the Sicilian kingdom by establishing family ties between Palermo and Constantinople. Cooperation with the Sicilian kingdom was especially desirable because relations between Venice and Byzantium were deteriorating.

During the negotiations with William I's widow, Queen Margaret, who was acting as regent for her young son William II, Manuel offered the hand of his daughter Maria to William. Since Maria was the former fiancée of Prince Béla and their engagement had been dissolved only in 1169, after the birth of Manuel's son Alexius, it is probable that the offer was not made earlier than 1169.[4]

The offer was accepted by the court of Palermo and Princess Maria was supposed to arrive at Taranto in the spring of 1172, to be greeted there by her prospective husband. At the last moment, however, Manuel apparently abandoned the marriage project and did not bother even to excuse himself at the Sicilian court. This attitude understandably caused strong resentment in Sicily and ruined Manuel's plan for cooperation with the Norman-Sicilian kingdom.[5]

The sources are silent about the motives behind this unexpected turn. Manuel's conduct can be explained only by the fact that in 1170 Frederick Barbarossa once more showed willingness to negotiate with the Byzantine emperor, and sent his personal envoy, Christian, archbishop of Mainz, to Constantinople. Manuel perhaps saw an opportunity to avoid or to postpone an open conflict with Barbarossa. At any rate, he entered into negotiations with the German emperor and proposed the marriage of Maria to Barbarossa's son Henry. Several embassies were exchanged between Manuel and Barbarossa in this matter and Manuel definitely abandoned the idea of a Byzantine-Norman alliance in the spring of 1172, when Maria's voyage to Taranto was cancelled without excuse.[6]

Manuel's decision might also have been motivated by the fact that in the spring of 1172 the Hungarian question suddenly became acute. King Stephen III, whose reign represented a rapprochement with Germany, died in March, 1172 and the succession opened for Manuel's protégé and brother-in-law, Béla III. The accession of Béla to the throne of Hungary evidently meant the return of Hungary to the Byzantine sphere of influence, a development which could have been opposed by the German emperor. In order to secure a smooth and swift change-over in Hungary and to establish a strong position for Byzantium in the Danube basin it was, therefore, essential that the negotiations initiated by Barbarossa in 1170 should not be broken off. This seems to be a fairly plausible explanation for Manuel's turnabout concerning Sicily. He had to choose immediately between two strongholds which were of primary importance for his future plans. One was Hungary, where the road to Byzantine control was open; the other was Italy, where Manuel intended to open an access through the prospective marriage of Maria and William II. At the moment it was the question of Hungary which needed immediate attention. The continuation of a rapprochement with Sicily would have meant a rupture with Barbarossa, and possibly a conflict with him over Hungary, which already seemed to be in Manuel's reach through the accession of Béla III. Therefore, the plan of a Sicilian alliance had to be sacrificed.[7]

Barbarossa's diplomacy did not lag behind Manuel's in duplicity. In 1173, while the negotiations with Byzantine were still going on, Barbarossa, aided by the Venetian fleet, attacked Ancona, an Adriatic city friendly to the *basileus*.[8] The German emperor also initiated negotiations with William II, the king of Norman-Sicily, for an alliance against Byzantium, an attempt which brought no positive results. In 1173 Barbarossa took up contacts also with Kilidj Arslan, the sultan of Iconium, in order to tie down important Byzantine forces in the East.[9]

It is not surprising that in this atmosphere of mutual distrust negotiations for a reconciliation between Manuel and Barbarossa had no prospects for success. Indeed, the last Byzantine embassy, which arrived in Regensburg in June, 1174 to discuss the proposed marriage of Henry and Maria, left without accomplishing its task.[10] The idea of a rapprochement with Barbarossa proved to be illusory and the net result of the negotiations with Germany was that Manuel missed the opportunity to form a Byzantine-Norman alliance against his chief rival in Italy.

The other setback which Manuel's foreign policy suffered in these years was the rupture with the republic of Venice. The republic, which during the earlier part of

Manuel's reign supported the *basileus* against the Normans in the battle for possession of the island of Corfù, more recently, in the question of Dalmatia, found her interests conflicting with those of Byzantium, particularly since Manuel, as a consequence of his wars against Stephen III, had succeeded in obtaining the cession of Dalmatia from Hungary, and had placed the theme of Dalmatia under direct Byzantine administration.[11] Tension increased when the Byzantine government, satisfying the general animosity caused by the monopolistic position of the Venetians in the commercial life of Byzantium, decided to cut short the privileges accorded to the Venetians. Moreover, it ordered the confiscation of large sums of money from the Venetian merchants as reprisal for alleged Venetian attacks against Genoese merchants residing in Constantinople.[12] Finally, in March, 1171, Manuel ordered the arrest of all Venetian subjects residing in Byzantine territory and confiscation of their possessions.[13]

Venice reacted with an immediate declaration of war against the empire and sent a fleet to attack the Dalmatian cities. Traù and Ragusa opened their gates and in the winter of 1171-1172 the Venetian fleet continued its operations in the Greek archipelago in the Aegean. In the spring of 1172, however, an epidemic broke out aboard the Venetian ships and the fleet was forced to return home. The punitive expedition thus ended in failure.[14]

After this incident the new doge of the republic, Sebastiano Ziani, entered into negotiations with Manuel for the release and compensation of the Venetian subjects. Apparently these negotiations remained unsuccessful during Manuel's reign. In 1175 the Venetians, disillusioned by their experiences with Byzantium, turned toward the equally disappointed Normans and a treaty of alliance was concluded with William II.[15]

The Norman-Venetian alliance was a serious blow to Manuel's western schemes. After 1175 Manuel could count only on the pope, Ancona, and the Lombard cities as allies in the competition with Barbarossa for control of Italy. If the victory of the Lombard League over Barbarossa on May 29, 1176 at Legnano seemingly turned the situation in Italy in favor of Manuel, the peace treaty of Venice in 1177 between Alexander III and Barbarossa significantly failed to mention the *basileus* among the allies of the pope. This omission seems to reflect not only a change in Alexander's attitude, for he was now reconciled with Barbarossa and less dependent on Byzantine support, but also the loss of prestige which Byzantium suffered in the previous year through the military disaster of Myriocephalon.[16]

After 1173, when the hostilities with Venice had already ended and the succession in Hungary following Stephen III's death was satisfactorily solved, Manuel had to turn his interest toward the affairs of Asia Minor. Kilidj Arslan, the sultan of Iconium, who by the treaty of 1162 was formally in alliance with the empire, repudiated the friendship and, perhaps at the instigation of Barbarossa, started negotiations with Nur-ed-din, the powerful *atabeg* of Mosul, against whom a Byzantine fleet in support of Amaury, king of Jerusalem, had fought an unsuccessful campaign in Egypt in 1169. Manuel also reproached the sultan for failing to return to the empire certain territories which had originally belonged to Byzantium.[17]

When Manuel's admonitions remained fruitless, the *basileus* decided to force Kilidj Arslan into obedience and in 1176 personally led a strong army against Iconium. The Turks retreated before the Byzantine army and lured it into a narrow mountain pass near the fort of Myriocephalon. Here, on September 17, 1176, the troops of Kilidj Arslan inflicted a crushing defeat on the Byzantines.[18] The

major part of the army perished; the emperor and but a
fraction of his troops escaped, thanks mainly to the fact
that Kilidj Arslan did not insist on complete annihilation
of the enemy. He was ready to conclude a new treaty on
fairly mild terms, asking only the destruction of certain
fortifications as well as the payment of a heavy contribu-
tion.[19]

The disaster of Myriocephalon was a severe blow not
only to the military power of Byzantium but even more
to the prestige of the Byzantine emperor. During the most
critical phase of the battle his usual courage seems to have
been shaken for the first time—for a moment he thought
of abandoning his soldiers and, clandestinely fleeing the
field.[20] In his first message to Constantinople announcing
the disaster, Manuel compared his defeat with that major
disaster of Byzantine history, the battle of Manzikert, lost
by the emperor Romanus IV.[21]

Nevertheless, on his return to the capital Manuel regained his self-confidence and evidently tried to minimize
the importance of his defeat. He refused to comply with
the conditions which were imposed upon him by Kilidj
Arslan, and hostilities with the Turks were resumed. In a
letter addressed to King Henry II of England giving a
description of the battle, Manuel tried to embellish the
facts and to give the impression that it was Kilidj Arslan
who asked for peace.[22]

He also resumed with the old persistence his diplomatic
activities concerning Italy and the West. Although the
treaty of Venice in 1177 ended the hostility between Germany, the Lombard communes, and the papacy which had
played an important role in his diplomatic combinations
against Barbarossa, Manuel tried to utilize a new discontent
which broke out in Lombardy, following the treaty of Venice, against the emperor's representative, Archbishop Chris-

tian of Mainz. The leader of the rebels was William, the marquis of Montferrat, whose son, Conrad, defeated and captured Christian in September, 1179. Manuel supported the rebellion financially and to seal his alliance with Montferrat, agreed to a marriage between William's other son Renier and his own daughter Maria. Renier of Montferrat was given the dignity of *caesar* and in February, 1180 the marriage was celebrated with great pomp in the palace of Blachernes.[23]

The unfortunate Princess Maria, who had already played the main role in Manuel's plans for marriage alliances with Béla of Hungary, William of Sicily, and Henry of Hohenstaufen, finally found her husband in the person of the young Italian aristocrat. His nomination for the dignity of *caesar* emphasized the political importance of the marriage because in 1171, on the occasion of the coronation of Alexius as co-emperor, Manuel had named Maria as second in the succession. Consequently, her husband Renier, who changed his name to John, would be claimant to the imperial throne if Alexius died without heirs.[24]

The marriage of Maria to Renier of Montferrat was soon followed by another political marriage plan reflecting the *basileus'* invariable interest in western political connections. Manuel was particularly anxious to establish closer ties with the Capetian dynasty and gain its support against the Hohenstaufen emperor. Pope Alexander III, who at the beginning of his pontificate strongly advocated an alliance of the western powers with Byzantium, as early as 1171 or 1172 advised Louis VII to bring about a union of the French royal house with the Comnenian dynasty.[25] But it was not until 1178 that Manuel decided to make a definite proposal to the French court. The occasion arrived when Philip of Alsace, count of Flanders, paid a visit to a Manuel in Constantinople while returning home from Palestine.

The emperor gave Philip a magnificent reception and asked him to convey a proposal for a marriage between his son and Louis VII's daughter. The count delivered the message. Shortly after, a Byzantine embassy arrived at the French court and officially presented Manuel's offer. Louis', reply was favorable. The little princess Agnes left Paris in the spring of 1179 and her betrothal with young Alexius was celebrated on March 2, 1180. The actual marriage was postponed until later since Alexius was only eleven years old and Agnes, who changed her name to Anna, but eight.[26]

This marriage was the *basileus'* last diplomatic success. He was already ill at the time of Agnes' arrival in Constantinople. His condition became more serious during the summer, which he spent outside the capital at Damelis, far away from state affairs and listening eagerly to the predictions of his astrologers, who promised him fourteen more years on the throne. In early September his condition became critical and even his indestructible optimism, which almost to the very end was forging ambitious schemes, abandoned him. With the end near, he seemed to realize the immensity and difficulties of the task which he left as inheritance to his young son.[27] Manuel died on September 24, 1180, and with him disappeared from the European political scene a man of strong vitality who had tried to rejuvenate the aging Byzantine world and steer it toward new horizons.

Manuel's prospects for the domination of Italy had already begun to fade during the last decade of his reign. And with his death his ambitious scheme of a union with the West disintegrated completely. Besides the violent disorders which beset the empire during the short-lived reign of Alexius II and the reign of terror under Andronicus, new storm clouds were gathering in the West. The reconciliation of Alexander III with Barbarossa in 1177 was followed several years later by the alliance of the German emperor with the king of Sicily, sealed in 1184 by the marriage of Barbarossa's son Henry and Constance, the daughter of Roger II and heiress to the Sicilian kingdom. In the following year, King William II of Sicily was able to take revenge for his humiliation by Manuel. He attacked and conquered Thessalonica, and this disaster brought Andronicus' reign to a sudden and bloody end. His successor, Isaac Angelus, had to face the problems and dangers of the Third Crusade, the conquest of Cyprus by Richard the Lionhearted, and a revolt of the Bulgarians and Serbians in the Balkans.[28]

In the general confusion that accompanied this decline of imperial power, it was only in Hungary that the balance established by Manuel remained at least temporarily in effect. King Béla III kept the situation stabilized; his only independent action was the recapture of Sirmium and the Dalmatian cities in the year following Manuel's death. These territories Béla considered his appanage though they had been kept under Byzantine administration even after his return to Hungary. Béla's action took place without bloodshed and to a certain extent it also served the interests of Byzantium, for it prevented the Dalmatian cities from falling under Venetian domination. The city of Zara was already under the control of the republic of Venice and had to be reconquered by force. In February, 1181, only a few months after Manuel's death, a Hungarian governor again resided in Zara. In 1193 the Venetians made an attempt to recapture the city, but the attack was unsuccessful.[29]

When Andronicus seized power in Byzantium in 1182 in the wake of a violent anti-Latin revolt, the Empress-Regent Marie of Antioch asked Béla III to intervene for the protection of the young Emperor Alexius II. According to Nicetas, this secret communication with the Hungarian court was held against the empress by Andronicus, who forced her to abandon the regency and banished her to a convent.[30] Béla started a campaign in alliance with the zupan of Rascia, Stephen Nemanja, which, however, came too late to attain its objective, the liberation of Alexius. Andronicus had begun by ordering the poisoning of Manuel's daughter Maria and her husband, Renier of Montferrat. The empress Marie of Antioch was condemned to death and strangled. In September, 1183, Andronicus proclaimed himself co-emperor, and young Alexius II was assassinated by his order a few months later. Andronicus then married Alexius' twelve-year-old bride, Princess Agnes-Anne Capet.[31]

While these events were occurring in Constantinople, Béla III occupied the towns of Belgrade and Branicevo on the Danube frontier, and proceeded into Byzantine territory as far as Nis and Sardica (Sophia). Hungarian troops occupied the valley of the Morava for three years.[32] Béla ended his campaign only after a popular revolt following the conquest of Thessalonica by the Normans in September, 1185 put an end to Andronicus' reign, and Isaac Angelus, a grandson of Alexius I, was proclaimed emperor.

According to modern Hungarian historians, Béla may have intended to take advantage of the extermination of Manuel's family by Andronicus to secure the Byzantine throne for himself. This assumption seems to be supported by the fact that Béla, whose wife, Anne of Châtillon, died in 1184, asked for the hand of Manuel's only surviving sister, the widowed Princess Theodora, who was leading the life of a nun in a convent. Through this marriage Béla eventually could have realized Manuel's old plan for a personal union between Byzantium and Hungary.[33] After the accession of Isaac Angelus, however, Béla recognized the new emperor, and soon established close family ties by giving him his daughter Margaret in marriage.[34] As proof of his good intentions, Béla also evacuated the occupied Byzantine provinces and withdrew his troops beyond the Danube. Isaac on his part acquiesced in the loss of the Dalmatian cities.[35]

After the accession of Isaac Angelus, Béla apparently gave up all plans to secure the Byzantine throne for himself, if he ever had such plans, and sought instead to strengthen the ties between Hungary and the West. In 1186 he married Margaret Capet, the sister of King Philip Augustus of France. Emeric, Béla's son and presumptive heir, was engaged to Barbarossa's daughter, and after her death married Constance, the daughter of King Alfonso of Aragon. When Barbarossa passed through Hungary on the Third Crusade, an engagement was arranged between his younger son, Duke Frederick of Swabia, and Béla's daughter, Constance.[36]

Béla also maintained friendly relations with Byzantium and on several occasions proved to be a staunch ally of his son-in-law, the Byzantine emperor. When Barbarossa was Béla's guest during his passage through Hungary, Béla accompanied him to the Byzantine border and mediated very effectively in the difficult negotiations with Isaac Angelus, who first refused to grant free passage for the German crusader army. Thus Béla averted a conflict between the two emperors. In 1195, the last year of his reign, Béla was ready to support Isaac in a campaign against the Bulgarians, but the planned common action was prevented by Isaac's deposition brought about by a military revolt in April, 1195. Béla was unable to save his son-in-law, imprisoned and blinded at the orders of his brother Alexius III, who had seized the Byzantine throne.[37]

Béla III died on April 23, 1196, and the close cooperation between Byzantium and Hungary came to an end. During the decade which followed his death, not only the Byzantine-Hungarian alliance but all contacts between the two countries were disrupted. This was primarily due to the rise of independent Slav states in the Balkans, Serbia and Bulgaria, which after the beginning of the thirteenth century isolated Hungary from Byzantium, and also to the disastrous events of the Fourth Crusade, which ended the power of the dynasty of the Angeli and established a Latin empire in Constantinople.

Conclusion

THE Hungarian kingdom during the first two hundred years of its existence in the Danube basin had frequently been exposed to the influence of the Byzantine Empire, either through peaceful contacts or more often in the form of armed conflicts. The strategic importance of the Balkans and the need for constant vigilance along the Danube frontier, had been recognized by the emperors of Byzantium even before the first Hungarian settlements were established north of the Danube.

The importance of the Danube frontier and the interest in Hungarian affairs became more pronounced during the twelfth century, especially under the Emperor Manuel Comnenus, who deliberately sought to establish Byzantine control, in one form or other, over Hungary. His efforts were closely related to his general political scheme aimed at the expansion of Byzantine imperial authority to Italy, and even perhaps the unification of Italy and Byzantium in a revived Roman Empire under Byzantine auspices.

Modern historians have regarded Manuel's chimerical dreams of imperial restoration as inspired by the example of Justinian. The collapse of Manuel's schemes and of the Byzantine Empire itself have been attributed to his unwarranted interest in western affairs. This, it is argued, led to the neglect of the East, where the collapse of the empire really started.[1] While it is certainly true that Manuel's interest in the West, his favoritism towards the Latins, and his costly wars and diplomacy roused strong dissatisfaction among his subjects and led to disastrous consequences after his death, it is also undeniable that powerful historical forces, not merely personal ambition, determined Manuel's policies.

Nicetas, who in his *History* is often critical of Manuel's actions, gives a different interpretation of Manuel's foreign policy in the seventh book of his work about Manuel's reign, written from a perspective of about twenty-five years and in the light of the experiences of the Fourth Crusade. Here Nicetas views the *basileus'* particular interest in western affairs not merely as an imperialistic desire to expand the power of Byzantium, but rather as a defensive move to prevent the kings of western Europe from forming an alliance against the *Romans* (i.e., Byzantium) under the leadership of a major power, perhaps the German emperor. The *basileus* therefore offered several of these western rulers his aid to enable them to resist any temptation to enter such an alliance against Byzantium.[2]

Perhaps Nicetas, as a contemporary historian, felt more directly the power of the compelling historical forces which inevitably placed the Byzantine Empire on a path where it would encounter the challenge posed by the West. He was able to perceive political foresight among Manuel's motives along with personal ambition. Manuel was facing a newly vigorous, expanding western Europe whose interests since the First Crusade were focused on the East, on the Latin states of Syria and Palestine, natural spheres of interest and former provinces of the Byzantine Empire.

This situation already existed during the reign of the early Comnenians, but it became much more important under Manuel because of new factors which emerged during his reign. One was the rising power of the Hohenstaufens, which had two natural lines of expansion—one towards

Italy, the other through the Danube basin to the Adriatic and to the Balkans. The other factor was the Norman-Sicilian kingdom which, annexing Apulia and Calabria under Roger II, also directed its expansion toward the Balkans. A third danger was added by the Moslems, once divided under several minor princes, but united under such strong leaders as Kilidj Arslan, Nur-ed-din, and Saladin during the second half of the twelfth century. Thenceforth the Moslems constituted a serious threat not only to the Latin states of the Near East, but to the Byzantine Empire itself.

Placed between these threats and unable to maintain self-sufficient isolation, the Comnenian emperors, and Manuel first among them, were fatally committed to following a western political course and seeking the Byzantine Empire's future, perhaps even its very survival, in its integration with western Europe. In his efforts to reunite Byzantium with the West, Manuel can hardly be blamed for refusing to surrender the leadership to the new rising power of the Honhenstaufens, and for trying to maintain and preserve the role which had been accorded to him through the ancient heritage and traditions of *Romania*.

In the power contest which arose for the control of Italy, Manuel very soon came to recognize the political and military importance of Hungary and the Balkans. His first great military action against the Normans in 1147-49 had to be delayed because of the unrest of the Serbs in the Balkans, who in turn had been aided by Hungary. Thereafter Manuel sought first to secure the northern frontier of the empire against possible enemy attacks. This, however, required much more time and effort than was foreseen. Manuel became more and more involved in the internal affairs and succession disputes of Hungary and he launched no fewer than ten attacks in a period of twenty-two years until he succeeded in establishing permanent Byzantine influence in Hungary with the accession of his brother-in-law Béla III to the Hungarian throne in 1175.

While Manuel's efforts in Hungary ultimately were crowned with success, the campaigns which secured control of Hungary prevented him from exerting the necessary military effort in Italy, the area of paramount Byzantine interests and aspirations, where all his military and political efforts should have been concentrated. When he finally established a strong position for Byzantium in the Balkans and in Hungary and was free to take decisive action in Italy, the complexity of the Italian situation, his own political blunders with regard to Venice and Norman Sicily, and the military disaster of Myriocephalon combined to offset the effects of his Hungarian success. After Manuel's death there was no real power in Byzantium which could have made use of the Hungarian alliance. The empire, its forces already undermined through the long wars, started to disintegrate from within even before it received the final blow during the Fourth Crusade.

Thus the long struggle between Hungary and the Byzantine Empire, which on the part of Hungary was fought essentially to preserve the country's western orientation and heritage, was to a large extent responsible for the failure of Manuel's great design.

As far as Hungary is concerned, the gradual disengagement from the Byzantine alliance following Manuel's death was beneficial. Under Béla III Hungary regained its full freedom of action and Byzantine influence in Hungary came definitely to an end. Nothing proves better the political wisdom and foresight of this great ruler of medieval Hungary, brought up and trained in Byzantium, than Hungary's decisive and definite turn toward the West during his reign, for this had really been her national destiny since the foundation of the kingdom.

Many historians have seen in the closing of the twelfth century and the early part of the thirteenth an irreversible parting of the ways of Eastern and Western Christendom. In this development, so significant to the future of Europe, the roles of Hungary and the Byzantine Empire were typical and of the utmost importance.

Notes and References

CHAPTER ONE

1. For the prehistory of the Hungarians, see D. Sinor, *History of Hungary* (New York, 1959), pp. 15-22; D. Kosáry, *A History of Hungary* (Cleveland-New York, 1941), pp. 7-18; also C. A. Macartney, *The Magyars in the Ninth Century* (Cambridge, 1930); H. Schönebaum, *Die Kenntnisse der byzantinischen Geschichtsschreiber von der ältesten Geschichte der Ungarn vor der Landnahme* (Leipzig-Berlin, 1922); *The Cambridge Medieval History* (Cambridge, 1966), IV, 566-569.

2. For further details, see L. Bréhier, *Le monde byzantin. Vie et mort de Byzance* (Paris, 1947); G. Ostrogorsky, *History of the Byzantine State*, trans. J. Hussey (Oxford, 1956).

3. Concerning Byzantine moves against the Arabs under Michael III and Basil I see Bréhier, *op. cit.*, pp. 130-131; Ostrogorsky, *op. cit.*, pp. 201, 209-211; A. A. Vasiliev, *Byzance et les Arabes* (Brussels, 1935), I, 251ff; J. Gay, *L'Italie méridionale et l'Empire Byzantin depuis l'avènement de Basil Ier jusqu'à la prise de Bari par les Normands, 867-1071* (Paris, 1904), pp. 79-101.

4. Ostrogorsky, *op. cit.*, p. 209.

5. Bréhier, *op. cit.*, p. 130.

6. *Ibid.*, p. 111.

7. A. A. Vasiliev, *History of the Byzantine Empire* (Madison, 1958), p. 326.

8. Bréhier, *op. cit.*, p. 235.

9. F. Chalandon, *Essai sur le règne d'Alexis Ier Comnène* (Paris, 1900), p. 8.

10. Bréhier, *loc. cit.*

11. Bréhier, *op. cit.*, pp. 147-148; Ostrogorsky, *op. cit.*, pp. 226-227. The first reliable contemporary source dealing with the appearance of the Hungarians on the European scene is the account of the Emperor Constantine VII Porphyrogenitus, son of Leo VI. His treatise about the imperial administration contains information concerning the relations of the empire with its neighbors, among them the Hungarians, whom he consistently calls Türks. See *De Administrando Imperio*, Greek text ed. by Gy. Moravcsik, English trans. by R. J. H. Jenkins (Budapest, 1949).

12. *The Cambridge Medieval History*, IV, 566-569; Vasiliev, *History of the Byzantine Empire*, I, 324.

13. Sinor, *op. cit.*, p. 18.

14. While Arnulf's emperorship was only a short-lived episode, after the coronation of Otto I the subsequent German rulers consistently pursued the

policy of union of the German kingship with the imperial crown and were called emperors. Their domains included Germany and northern and central Italy. Cf. G. Barraclough, *The Origins of Modern Germany* (New York, 1963), pp. 46-71.

15. Sinor, *op. cit.*, pp. 18-28; Kosáry, *op. cit.*, p. 10.

16. Sinor, *op. cit.*, pp. 42-43.

17. Bréhier, *op. cit.*, pp. 168, 187; A. Rambaud, *L'empire grec au dixième siècle. Constantin Porphyrogenète* (Paris, 1870), pp. 358, 361-363; Sinor, *op. cit.*, p. 29.

18. B. Hóman, *Geschichte des ungarischen Mittelalters* (Berlin, 1940-43), I, 164.

19. Sinor, *op. cit.*, p. 38.

20. Bréhier, *op. cit.*, pp. 266-281; Ostrogorsky, *op. cit.*, pp. 304-305; F. Chalandon, *Histoire de la domination normande en Italie* (Paris, 1907), I, 184-190; P. Charanis, "The Byzantine Empire in the Eleventh Century," *A History of the Crusades,* ed. K. Setton and M. Baldwin (Philadelphia, 1955), I, 193-201.

21. H. Marczali, *History of Hungary in the Age of the Arpáds* (in Hungarian, Budapest, 1896), p. 62; Bréhier, *op. cit.*, p. 277. For the presence of the Pechenegs in Byzantine territory and the actions of Isaac Comnenus, see M. Psellus, *Chronographia,* VII, 67-70, ed. and Eng. trans. E. R. A. Sewter (New Haven, 1953), pp. 241-243; J. Scylitzes, *Historia,* 645, 646, ed. Migne, *Patrologia Graeca,* CXXII.

22. Ostrogorsky, *op. cit.*, p. 303; *Chronicon Pictum Marci de Kalt* (Chronicon Pictum Vindobonense), 104-109, ed. and Hungarian trans. L. Geréb (Budapest, 1959), pp. 133-137; *Chronicon Posoniense,* ed. Endlicher, *Rerum Hungaricarum Monumenta Arpadiana* (Sangalli, 1849), p. 56.

23. Cinnamus, *Historia,* 5.8.227, ed. Migne, *Patrologia Graeca,* CXXXIII; *Chronicon Pictum,* 111-112.

24. *Chronicon Pictum,* 110; H. Mügeln, *Chronicon,* 38, ed. E. Szentpétery, *Scriptores Rerum Hungaricarum* (Budapest, 1937), II.

25. Marczali, *op. cit.*, p. 93.

26. For details on Gregory VII, see A. Fliche, *La réforme grégorienne et la reconquête Chrétienne (1057-1123),* Vol. VIII of *Histoire de l'Eglise depuis les origines jusqu'à nos jours,* ed. A. Fliche and V. Martin (Paris, 1938-1952), pp. 65-66, 110-118.

27. Ph. Jaffe (ed.), *Regesta Pontificum Romanorum,* 4886, 4944, 4952 (Leipzig, 1885), I, 608, 613, 614.

28. Marczali, *op. cit.*, p. 105.

29. *Ibid.;* See also F. Dölger, "Ungarn in der byzantinischen Reichspolitik," *Archivum Europae Centro-Orientalis,* VIII, 3-4 (1942), 329-331.

30. *Chronicon Pictum,* 133.

31. Jaffe, *Regesta,* 5036, I, 622; Fliche-Martin, *op. cit.*, VIII, 121.

32. Bernold of Constance, *Chronicon,* ed. Scheffer, *Monumenta Germaniae Historica Scriptores,* V, 456, quoted in Marczali, *op. cit.*, pp. 134-135.

33. Ostrogorsky, *op. cit.*, p. 305.

34. In this area the doge of Venice represented the authority of the Byzantine emperor since 998 as Dux Dalmatiae, fighting against frequent incursions of the Croatian princes. Cf. Chalandon, *Essai sur le règne d'Alexis Comnène,* p. 8. For the early history of Dalmatia, see also L. Vojnovich, *Histoire de*

Dalmatie (2 vols.; Paris, 1934); G. Novak, *Proslost Dalmacije* ("The Past of Dalmatia") (2 vols., in Croatian; Zagreb, 1944).
  35. Ostrogorsky, *op. cit.,* p. 277.
  36. *Ibid.,* p. 306; Bréhier, *op. cit.,* p. 285; Fliche-Martin, *op. cit.,* VIII, 112, 121.
  37. J. Thuroczy, *Chronica Hungarorum,* II, 56, ed. J. Schwandtner, *Scriptores Rerum Hungaricarum Veteres* (Vienna, 1746-48), I.
  38. Jaffé, *Regesta,* no. 5662 (dated July 27, 1096). Marczali thinks that this date is incorrect and that the letter was probably written in 1095, the year of Ladislas' death, because in the following year the pope would have mentioned the crusade which had passed through Hungary. Cf. Marczali, *op. cit.,* p. 183.
  39. *Monumenta Bambergensia,* 88, ed. Jaffé, *Bibliotheca Rerum Germanicarum* (Berlin, 1869), V, 172-173.
  40. Marczali, *op. cit.,* p. 190; Fliche-Martin, *op. cit.,* VIII, 319.
  41. Cf. S. Runciman, *A History of the Crusades* (Cambridge, 1951), I; F. Duncalf, "The First Crusade: Clermont to Constantinople," *A History of the Crusades,* ed. K. Setton and M. Baldwin (Philadelphia, 1955), I, 259-262, 265, 268-269; S. Büchler, *Ungarn während und nach der Kreuzzugsperiode* (New York, 1909), pp. 4-13.

CHAPTER TWO

  1. Marczali, *op. cit.,* pp. 200-202.
  2. Coloman yielded to the papal point of view on the question of lay investiture and solemnly renounced the right to appoint bishops. During his reign two synods were held in Hungary, both convoked by the legate of Pope Pascal II. These synods emphatically denounced simony and, in the question of celibacy of the clergy, fully asserted the papal views; cf. Marczali, *op. cit.,* pp. 228-233; Sinor, *op. cit.,* p. 50; Fliche-Martin, *op. cit.,* VIII, 319.
  3. Thuroczy, *Chronica Hungarorum,* II, 56-60; H. Marczali, *Les relations de la Dalmatie et de la Hongrie du XIe au XIIe siècle* (Paris, 1899), p. 9; F. Dvornik, *The Slavs: Their Early History and Civilization* (Boston, 1956), p. 278; G. Novak, *op. cit.,* I, 115.
  4. Marczali, *History of Hungary in the Age of the Arpáds,* p. 208.
  5. Thuroczy, *Chronica,* II, 60.
  6. For Alexius' reign, his internal and external policies in general, the most comprehensive treatment is provided by Chalandon, *Essai sur le règne d'Alexis I Comnène* (Paris, 1900). Cf. also P. Charanis, "The Byzantine Empire in the 11th Century," *A History of the Crusades,* ed. Setton-Baldwin, I, 214; Bréhier, *op. cit.,* p. 300.
  7. Fliche-Martin, *op. cit.,* VIII, 69-70; Bréhier, *op. cit.,* p. 291; Vasiliev, *History of the Byzantine Empire,* I, 358, II, 395-396.
  8. Bréhier, *op. cit.,* pp. 307-308; Charanis, *loc. cit.,* pp. 216-217; Chalandon, *Essai sur le règne d'Alexis,* pp. 62-65; S. Runciman, *The Eastern Schism* (Oxford, 1955), pp. 59-62.
  9. Ch. Diehl, *History of the Byzantine Empire,* trans. G. B. Ives (Princeton, 1925), pp. 122-124; S. Runciman, "The First Crusade: Antioch to Ascalon," *A History of the Crusades,* ed. K. Setton and M. Baldwin (Phila-

delphia, 1955), I, 309 ff; H. S. Fink, "The Foundation of the Latin States, 1099-1118," *A History of the Crusades,* ed. Setton-Baldwin, I, 372 ff; Chalandon, *Essai sur le règne d'Alexis Comnène,* pp. 199-203, 233-234.

10. Chalandon, *Essai sur le règne d'Alexis,* pp. 236-237; Bréhier, *op. cit.,* pp. 314-316.

11. Anna Comnena, *Alexiad,* trans. E. Dawes (London, 1928), XIII, 9-12, XIV, 2; cf. Chalandon, *Essai sur le règne d'Alexis,* pp. 246-253.

12. Anna Comnena, *Alexiad,* XIII, 12; Chalandon, *Essai sur le règne d'Alexis Comnène,* p. 249; Ostrogorsky, *op. cit.,* pp. 324-325.

13. Cinnamus, *Historia,* I, 4, 10, *Patrologia Graeca,* CXXXIII; Chalandon, *Jean II Comnène et Manuel I Comnène,* I, 28.

14. *The Russian Primary Chronicle, Laurentian Text,* ed. and trans. S. H. Cross and O. P. Sherbowitz-Wetzor (Cambridge, Mass., 1953), p. 202.

15. Otto of Freising, *Chronicon,* VII, 13, ed. R. Wilmans, *Monumenta Germaniae Historica Scriptores* (Hannover, 1868), XX.

16. *Chronicon Pictum,* 149, ed. and trans. L. Geréb, p. 168; Chalandon, *Jean Comnène et Manuel Comnène,* I, 62.

17. *Chronicon Pictum,* 150; Otto of Freising, *Chronicon,* VII, 21.

18. G. Fejér, *Codex Diplomaticus Hungariae* (Budae, 1829), II, 151.

19. Cf. Chalandon, *Jean Comnène et Manuel Comnène,* I, 56.

20. The names of Oliver and Rathold, Norman noblemen from Caserta, are mentioned as being in the company of the king; cf. Marczali, *History of Hungary,* pp. 255-256.

21. Dandolo, *Chronicon Venetum,* ed. Muratori, *Rerum Italicarum Scriptores* (Milan, 1723), XII, 266; Chalandon, *Jean Comnène et Manuel Comnène,* I, 56.

22. Marczali, *History of Hungary,* p. 256.

23. Thuroczy, *Chronica Hungarorum,* I, 172-176.

24. Cinnamus, *Historia,* VI, 10; Chalandon, *Jean Comnène et Manuel Comnène,* I, 156-158; Ostrogorsky, *op. cit.,* p. 335.

25. Nicetas Choniates, *Historia,* 23, ed. Migne, *Patrologia Graeca* CXXXIX; Ch. Diehl, *op. cit.,* pp. 114 ff.

26. Ostrogorsky, *op. cit.,* p. 335; Chalandon, *Jean Comnène et Manuel Comnène,* I, 65-76.

27. Fliche-Martin, *op. cit.,* IX, Part I, pp. 49-50; E. Caspar, *Roger II (1101-1154) und die Gründung der normannisch-sizilischen Monarchie* (Innsbruck, 1904), pp. 92-97; cf. also E. Curtis, *Roger of Sicily and the Normans in Lower Italy, 1016-1154* (New York-London, 1912).

28. Cinnamus, *Historia,* II, 4, 36; Otto of Freising, *The Deeds of Frederick Barbarossa,* I, 24, ed. and trans. C. C. Mierow (New York, 1953), p. 54; W. Ohnsorge, "Die Bedeutung der deutsch-byzantinischen Beziehungen im 12. Jahrhundert für den deutschen Osten," *Abendland und Byzanz,* ed. W. Ohnsorge (Darmstadt, 1958), p. 437.

29. Thuroczy, *Chronica,* II, 63; Dandolo, *Chronicon,* ed. Muratori, *Rerum Italicarum Scriptores,* XII, 270-271; Chalandon, *Jean Comnène et Manuel Comnène,* I, 57.

30. Chalandon, *loc. cit.;* Marczali, *History of Hungary,* p. 261. It should be noted that Almos was Coloman's younger brother and therefore uncle of Stephen II. Ostrogorsky erroneously calls him Stephen II's brother (cf. Ostrogorsky, *op. cit.,* p. 336). A similar error is commited by Diehl, who calls the

young Prince Béla, who was also blinded, "son of the dethroned King Coloman." Béla was son of Almos and therefore Coloman's nephew. Coloman, by the way, was never dethroned; he was succeeded by his son, Stephen II; cf. Diehl, *op. cit.,* p. 115.

31. Thuroczy, *Chronica Hungarorum,* II, 63; Chalandon, *Jean Comnène et Manuel Comnène,* I, 61; Marczali, *History of Hungary,* p. 261.
32. Nicetas, *Historia,* 24. According to the *Annales Posonienses,* ed. E. Szentpétery, *Scriptores Rerum Hungaricarum* (Budapest, 1937), I, 119-127, the Hungarians conquered Nis in 1127.
33. Cinnamus, *Historia,* I, 4, 10; Chalandon, *Jean Comnène et Manuel Comnène,* I, 58.
34. Nicetas, *Historia,* 25; Thuroczy, *Chronica,* II, 63.
35. Cinnamus, *Historia,* I, 4, 10; Marczali, *History of Hungary,* p. 262; Chalandon, *Jean Comnène et Manuel Comnène,* I, 59-61.
36. Canonici *Wisegradensis Continuatio Cosmae,* ed. Köpke, *Monumenta Germaniae Historica Scriptores,* IX, 143; cf. Marczali, *History of Hungary,* p. 266.
37. Thuroczy, *Chronica,* II, 63-64; Otto of Freising, *Chronicon,* VII, 21.
38. Cinnamus, *Historia,* III, 11, 117; Otto of Freising, *Chronicon,* VII, 21.
39. Cinnamus, V, 6, 216; Chalandon, *Jean Comnène et Manuel Comnène,* I, 63.
40. Marczali, *History of Hungary,* p. 266.
41. Sinor, *History of Hungary,* p. 52. While it is correct to say that Hungary in her expansion to the Adriatic and in the northern Balkans leaned heavily on the independence movements of the Slavonic peoples in this area and gradually drew the Croats and Serbians away from the Byzantine orbit, it seems rather an overstatement to imply that Hungary played the role of a leading power in a larger Slavonic bloc. The incorporation of Croatia and later Rama or Bosnia did not transform Hungary into a "Slavonic power," as Chalandon puts it. ("La Hongrie, devenue puissance slave par l'annexion de la Croatie, ait cherché à grouper autour d'elle les peuples de race slave pour tenter de les opposer à Byzance"); cf. Chalandon, *Jean Comnène et Manuel Comnène,* p. 75. For Hungary's role among the southern Slavs, see F. Dvornik, *The Slavs: Their Early History,* p. 283.
42. Thuroczy, *Chronica Hungarorum,* II, 64; Otto of Freising, *Chronicon,* VII, 21.
43. *Herbordi Dialogus de vita Ottonis episcopi Babenbergensis,* I, 38, ed. R. Köpke, *Monumenta Germaniae Historica Scriptores* (Hannover, 1868), XX, 718; for the relations between Germany and Hungary under Conrad III, see Ohnsorge, *op. cit.,* p. 438.
44. Fejér, *Codex Diplomaticus Hungariae,* II, 39, 82; M. Asztalos and S. Pethö, *History of the Hungarian Nation,* in Hungarian (Budapest, 1934), p. 44; Chalandon, *Jean Comnène et Manuel Comnène,* I, 75; Dvornik, *op cit.,* p. 283.
45. William of Tyre, *Historia rerum in partibus transmarinis gestarum,* XV, 19, 20, *Recueil des historiens des croisades. Historiens occidentaux* (Paris, 1869-81), I, 689-690; Chalandon, *op. cit.,* I, 147-150, 187; Bréhier, *op. cit.,* pp. 322-324.
46. Cinnamus, *Historia,* I, 10, 24; Nicetas, *Historia,* 54.
47. Marczali, *History of Hungary,* pp. 286-287.

CHAPTER THREE

1. See above, pp. 27-28.

2. Joannes Lucius, *De regno Dalmatiae et Croatiae*, ed. J. Schwandtner, *Scriptores Rerum Hungaricarum Veteres* (Vienna, 1746-1748), III, 300-301; Diocleas Presbyter, *Regnum Slavorum* (*Ljetopis Popa Dukljanina*), ed. and trans. in Croatian by V. Mosin (Zagreb, 1950), XI-XV; Chalandon, *Jean Comnène et Manuel Comnène*, I, 65-76.

3. For the medieval history of the Serbs and their relations with Hungary, see also L. Thalloczy, "Die ungarischen Beziehungen der Chronik des Presbyter Diocleas," *Archiv für slavische Philologie*, XX (1898), 217-220; W. Miller, "The Medieval Serbian Empire," *The Quarterly Review*, 226 (July-October, 1916), 488-507; V. Laurent, "La Serbie entre Byzance et la Hongrie à la veille de la quatrième croisade," *Revue historique du sud-est européen*, XVIII (Bucharest, 1941), 109-130. Dvornik, *op. cit.*, pp. 279 ff.

4. Cinnamus, *Historia*, III, 6, 101; Chalandon, *Jean Comnène et Manuel Comnène*, II, 401; Marczali, *History of Hungary*, p. 289.

5. Ohnsorge, "Die Bedeutung der deutsch-byzantinischen Beziehungen im 12. Jahrhundert," *Abendland und Byzanz*, p. 441.

6. Cinnamus, *Historia*, II, 1, 29.

7. As younger son of John II, Manuel was not prepared to inherit his father's throne, and at the time of his accession he had to fear a possible attempt to contest his inheritance by two members of his family. His uncle, the Sebastocrator Isaac Comnenus, and his own elder brother, also called Isaac, could raise valid claims to the throne. Manuel did not hesitate to arrest his brother temporarily, and to send his uncle into exile until he felt himself secure on the throne; cf. Nicetas, *Historia*, I, 1, 65-67; Cinnamus, *Historia*, II, 1, 29, and II, 2, 32.

8. Cinnamus, *op. cit.*, II, 7, 49-51.

9. Diehl, *History of the Byzantine Empire*, pp. 111-136; Chalandon, *Jean Comnène et Manuel Comnène*, I, 205-206.

10. Chalandon, *Jean Comnène et Manuel Comnène*, I, 203, 308.

11. *Ibid.*, II, 555-558; Ostrogorsky, *op. cit.*, p. 338; Vasiliev, *History of the Byzantine Empire*, II, 431.

12. Cf. M. W. Baldwin, "The Latin States under Baldwin III and Amalric I," *A History of the Crusades*, ed. K. Setton and M. W. Baldwin (Philadelphia, 1955), I, 528ff; Diehl, *op. cit.*, pp. 116-118.

13. Cinnamus, *Historia*, II, 6, 45-46; Nicetas, *Historia*, I, 2, 72; Chalandon, *Jean Comnène et Manuel Comnène*, I, 239-255.

14. Cinnamus, *op. cit.*, II, 8, 59; S. Runciman, *History of the Crusades*, II, 266; Chalandon, *Jean Comnène et Manuel Comnène*, I, 253-257.

15. Cinnamus, *Historia*, VI, 7, 271-272; Chalandon, *Jean Comnène et Manuel Comnène*, II, 461-462, 489.

16. Diehl, *op. cit.*, pp. 116-118; Chalandon, *Jean Comnène et Manuel Comnène*, II, 467, 509-515.

17. Chalandon, *Jean Comnène et Manuel Comnène*, I, 172; Caspar, *Roger II und die Gründung der normannisch-sizilischen Monarchie*, pp. 362-364.

18. Cinnamus, *Historia*, II, 4, 36-37; cf. Chalandon, *Histoire de la domination normande en Italie et en Sicile* (Paris, 1907), II, 24, 127; Chalandon, *Jean Comnène et Manuel Comnène*, I, 197-98.

19. P. Lamma, *Comneni e Staufer* (Roma, 1955), I, 49-50; Chalandon, *Jean Comnène et Manuel Comnène*, I, 258-259.

20. Chalandon, *Jean Comnène et Manuel Comnène*, I, 259.

21. Cinnamus, *Historia*, III, 2, 92.

22. Cf. Otto of Freising, *The Deeds of Frederick Barbarossa*, I, 25(24), ed. and trans. C. C. Mierow (New York, 1953), pp. 57-58; Chalandon, *loc. cit.*

23. For the negotiations between the German and Byzantine courts and concerning Conrad's complaints see Lamma, *op. cit.*, I, 50-51; cf. also W. Bernhardi, *Konrad III* (Leipzig, 1883), pp. 410-416; Chalandon, *Jean Comnène et Manuel Comnène*, I, 259-262.

24. Anna Comnena draws the following picture of the participants in the First Crusade: "The simpler-minded were urged on by the real desire of worshipping at our Lord's Sepulchre . . . , but the more astute, especially men like Bohemond had another reason, namely the hope that while on their travels, they might by some means be able to seize the capital itself, finding a pretext for this." *Alexiad*, X, 5, trans. E. Dawes.

25. Chalandon, *Jean Comnène et Manuel Comnène*, I, 266-67.

26. V. G. Berry, "The Second Crusade," *A History of the Crusades*, ed. K. Setton and M. Baldwin (Philadelphia, 1955), I, 463-470; J. G. Rowe, "The Papacy and the Greeks (1122-1153)," reprinted from *Church History*, XXVIII, 3 (September, 1959), 11.

27. Odo of Deuil, *De profectione Ludovici VII in orientem*, I, ed. and trans. V. G. Berry (New York, 1948), p. 11.

28. Berry, "The Second Crusade," *A History of the Crusades*, ed. Setton and Baldwin, I, 483.

29. Otto of Freising, *Chronicon*, VII, 34, ed. R. Wilmans, *Monumenta Germaniae Historica Scriptores* (Hannover, 1868), XX; Odo of Deuil, *op. cit.*, II, 35.

30. *Chronicon Pictum*, ed. Geréb (Budapest, 1959), p. 166; Thuroczy, *Chronica Hungarorum*, ed. Schwandtner (Vienna, 1746), II, 66.

31. Thuroczy, *op. cit.*, II, 146; Odo of Deuil, *op. cit.*, II, 37; Marczali, *History of Hungary*, pp. 282-283; Bernhardi, *Konrad III*, p. 606; S. Büchler, *Ungarn während und nach der Kreuzzugsperiode* (New York, 1909), pp. 18-19.

32. Cinnamus, *Historia*, II, 12, 67-69.

33. For the passage of the crusaders and the difficulties with the Byzantine court, first hand information is in Odo of Deuil, *op. cit.*, Bks III-IV; William of Tyre, *Historia rerum*, XVI, 23; cf. Lamma, *op. cit.*, I, 70-74; Chalandon, *Jean Comnène et Manuel Comnène*, I, 277-79, 294-300.

34. Nicetas, *Historia*, II, 1, 98-102.

35. Dandolo, *Chronicon*, ed. Muratori, *Rerum Italicarum Scriptores* (Milan, 1723), XII, 281; cf. Chalandon, *Jean Comnène et Manuel Comnène*, I, 321-322.

36. Cinnamus, *Historia*, III, 3, 93.

37. *Ibid.*, II, 19, 87; cf. Chalandon, *Jean Comnène et Manuel Comnène*, I, 327.

38. Chalandon, *Jean Comnène et Manuel Comnène*, I, 334-335; *Cambridge Medieval History*, V, 357-58.

39. Cinnamus, *Historia*, III, 6, 101-102, 104.

40. Cf. Chalandon, *Jean Comnène et Manuel Comnène*, I, 337-342; Chalandon, *Histoire de la domination normande en Italie*, II, 119-120; Rowe, *op. cit.*, pp. 28-30, 67.

CHAPTER FOUR

1. *Chronicon Pictum,* ed. Geréb (Budapest, 1959), p. 157.
2. Chalandon, *Jean Comnène et Manuel Comnène,* II, 400; C. Grot, *Iz istorii Ugrij i Slavianstva v XII. vieke* ("From the History of the Hungarians and Slavs in the Twelfth Century"), in Russian (Warsaw, 1889), pp. 94-96; Marczali, *History of Hungary,* p. 283.
3. Chalandon, *Jean Comnène et Manuel Comnène,* II, 400; N. Karamzin, *Histoire de l'empire de Russie,* trans. St. Thomas and Jauffret (Paris, 1819-1826), II, 275.
4. Cinnamus, *Historia,* III, 10, 115; Chalandon, *loc. cit.*
5. I. Sharanevich, *Istoria Galichko-Volodimirskoj Rusi do roke 1453* ("History of Halich-Volodimirski Rus till 1453"), in Russian (Lvov, 1863), pp. 40-51; *Povest vremennych let, Ipatievskii spisok* ("Russian Primary Chronicle, Hypatios Version"), ed. Sachmatov (St. Petersburg, 1908); cf. Marczali, *History of Hungary,* p. 285.
6. Ferdinand Chalandon considers Hungary at this particular period as a Slavonic power and center of a league or bloc of Slavonic nations: "Cette tendence de la politique hongroise . . . nous montre les efforts d'une Hongrie, devenue déjà puissance slave par ses conquêtes en Croatie et en Dalmatie, pour gagner les autres peuples slaves, ses voisins, afin de s'appuyer sur eux pour lutter contre les empereurs d'Occident et d'Orient . . . ," cf. Chalandon, *Jean Comnène et Manuel Comnène,* II, 399.
7. Ohnsorge, *op. cit.,* pp. 438-439.
8. Otto of Freising, *The Deeds of Frederick Barbarossa,* p. 55; Ohnsorge, *loc. cit.*
9. Otto of Freising, *Chronicon,* VII, 34, ed. Wilmans, *Monumenta Germaniae Historica Scriptores,* XX.
10. Otto of Freising, *The Deeds of Frederick,* pp. 64-69.
11. Marczali, *History of Hungary,* pp. 278-280.
12. *Ibid.,* p. 284.
13. Otto of Freising, *Chronicon, Continuatio Sanblasiana,* ed. R. Williams, *Monumenta Germaniae Historica Scriptores,* XX, 305; cf. P. Lamma, *op. cit.,* I, 90; Chalandon, *Jean Comnène et Manuel Comnène,* I, 308.
14. Cinnamus, *Historia,* III, 6, 101-102.
15. *Lietopis po ipatskomu spisku* ("Chronicle in Hypatios version"), ed. Archeographic Commission (St. Petersburg, 1871), cited in Chalandon, *Jean Comnène et Manuel Comnène, p.* 385.
16. Cinnamus, *Historia,* III, 7, 103; Nicetas, *Historia,* II, 6, 120.
17. Cinnamus, *Historia,* V, 16, 217; Marczali, *History of Hungary,* p. 284.
18. Cinnamus, *Historia,* III, 11, 115; Marczali, *History of Hungary,* p. 287.
19. Cinnamus, *Historia,* III, 11, 116-117.
20. Nicetas, *Historia,* II, 7, 123; Cinnamus, *Historia,* III, 11-12, 117-119.
21. For Frederick's political aims, see G. Barraclough, *History in a Changing World* (Oxford, 1956), p. 86; for his attitude towards Byzantium, see Lamma, *op. cit.,* I, 133-35.

Notes and References   139

22. Fliche-Martin, *op. cit.*, IX, Part II, 7; Chalandon, *Jean Comnène et Manuel Comnène*, I, 343-44; Lamma, *op. cit.*, I, 137-141.

23. H. Pelzer, *Friedrichs I von Hohenstaufen Politik gegenüber Dänemark, Polen und Ungarn* (Münster, 1906), p. 5.

24. Otto of Freising, *The Deeds of Frederick*, p. 119.

25. Ohnsorge, *op. cit.*, pp. 442-443.

26. Cinnamus, *Historia*, III, 12, 120. Lamma suggests that it was Manuel's concern over the renewed German interest in Hungary which prompted him to accept Géza's offer; see Lamma, *op. cit.*, I, 133.

27. Otto of Freising, *The Deeds of Frederick*, pp. 123-124; Wibald, Abbot of Corvey, *Epistolae*, ed. Ph. Jaffe, *Bibliotheca Rerum Germanicarum* (Berlin, 1864), I, No. 410; Chalandon, *Jean Comnène et Manuel Comnène*, I, 346; Ohnsorge, *op. cit.*, pp. 431-432; Lamma, *op. cit.*, I, 142.

28. Cinnamus, *Historia*, IV, 1, 135; Wibald, *Epistolae*, I, 424.

29. Cf. Chalandon, *Jean Comnène et Manuel Comnène*, I, 347; Barraclough, *op. cit.*, p. 84; Lamma, *op. cit.*, I, 145-147.

30. Nicetas, *Historia*, III, 1, 132; Chalandon, *Jean Comnène et Manuel Comnène*, II, 391.

31. Cinnamus, *Historia*, III, 6, 101; cf. also G. Wenzel, *Codex diplomaticus Arpadianus*, No. 30, *Monumenta Hungariae Historica Diplomataria* (Budapest, 1860-74), I, 63; cf. Chalandon, *Jean Comnène et Manuel Comnène*, II, 401; Marczali, *History of Hungary*, p. 289.

32. Cinnamus, *Historia*, III, 17, 126-127.

33. *Ibid.*, III, 18, 129-130.

34. Nicetas, *Historia*, III, 1, 133; cf. Chalandon, *Jean Comnène et Manuel Comnène*, II, 411.

35. Cinnamus, *Historia*, III, 19, 132.

36. Nicetas, *Historia*, II, 7, 124; Otto of Freising, *The Deeds of Frederick*, p. 168; Chalandon, *Jean Comnène et Manuel Comnène*, II, 413.

37. Cinnamus, *Historia*, III, 12, 119.

38. Otto of Freising, *The Deeds of Frederick*, pp. 154-55.

39. Cinnamus, *Historia*, IV, 2, 137-138, IV, 5, 146-147.

40. *Ibid.*, IV, 13, 168-169; Nicetas, *Historia*, II, 7, 125.

41. Fliche-Martin, *op. cit.*, IX, Part 2, 24-26; Lamma, *op. cit.*, I, 221-224.

42. Chalandon, *Jean Comnène et Manuel Comnène*, I, 370.

43. Lamma, *op. cit.*, I, 155; Lamma suggests a possible cooperation between William I and Géza II.

44. Otto of Freising, *The Deeds of Frederick*, p. 164.

45. *Ibid.*, p. 168; Chalandon, *Jean Comnène et Manuel Comnène*, I, 373.

46. Cinnamus, *Historia*, III, 19, 131, 133-134; Chalandon, *Jean Comnène et Manuel Comnène*, II, 414.

47. Marczali, *History of Hungary*, p. 292; Ohnsorge, *op. cit.*, pp. 446-447.

48. Cinnamus, *Historia*, V, 1, 203; Nicetas, *Historia*, IV, 1, 165; Marczali, *History of Hungary*, p. 294; Chalandon, in connection with the dispute between Géza and his brother Stephen, also mentions the departure of the Ban "Bela" from the Hungarian court. The person in question is evidently the Ban Belos, who acted as head of the government during the minority of Géza II, and around 1158 left Hungary, perhaps because he was among the partisans of the pretender Stephen. Belos, who was brother of the Serbian Zupan Pervoslav, went to Rascia, but after the death of Géza II

he returned again to Hungary. Cf. Chalandon, *Jean Comnène et Manuel Comnène*, II, 469-470.

49. Marczali, *History of Hungary*, p. 293.
50. Wenzel, *Codex Diplomaticus Arpadianus*, VI, 96, No. 52.
51. Fliche-Martin, *op. cit.*, IX, Part 2, 55-58; cf. also H. Reuter, *Geschichte Alexanders des Dritten und der Kirche seiner Zeit* (Leipzig, 1860-64), I, 107; M. Pacaut, *Alexandre III. Etude sur la conception du pouvoir pontifical* (Paris, 1956), pp. 119-122; W. Holtzmann, "Papst Alexander III und Ungarn," *Ungarische Jahrbücher*, VI (Budapest, 1926), 397-426.
52. Marczali, *History of Hungary*, p. 293.
53. Ohnsorge, *op. cit.*, pp. 449-450; B. Hóman-J. Szekfü, *Magyar Történet* ("History of Hungary"), in Hungarian (Budapest, 1938), I, 381.
54. Pacaut, *op. cit.*, pp. 233-239; Barraclough, *The Origins of Modern Germany*, pp. 169-170; Barraclough, *History in a Changing World*, pp. 74-89, 121.

CHAPTER FIVE

1. F. Dölger, *Corpus der griechischen Urkunden des Mittelalters und der neueren Zeit. Regesten der Kaiserurkunden des oströmischen Reiches von 565-1453* (München-Berlin, 1925), II, No. 1420; cf. Ohnsorge, *op. cit.*, pp. 447-449.
2. Fliche-Martin, *op. cit.*, IX, Part 2, 64-65.
3. Pacaut, *Alexandre III*, p. 113.
4. *Ibid.*, pp. 235-239.
5. The place of this meeting was not disclosed by Burchard. The five kings or rulers presumably are Louis VII, William I, Manuel, Géza II, and perhaps Pervoslav, the zupan of Rascia, or the duke of Welf; cf. Ohnsorge, *op. cit.*, pp. 449-450.
6. Pacaut, *op. cit.*, pp. 233-234; Fliche-Martin, *op. cit.*, IX, Part 2, pp. 129, 135-136; for the relations between Alexander III and Louis VII, see also Reuter, *Geschichte Alexanders des Dritten*, pp. 199-202, as well as M. Pacaut, "Louis VII et Alexandre III (1159-1180)," *Revue d'Histoire de l'Eglise de France*, XXXIX, 132 (Paris, 1953); Lamma, *op. cit.*, II, 123-143.
7. Cinnamus, *Historia*, VI, 4, 262; Chalandon, *Jean Comnène et Manuel Comnène*, II, 563-566.
8. When Alexander III induced the Lombard League to join the anti-German coalition and in 1166 sent a new archbishop to Milan to rebuild the city destroyed by Barbarossa, Manuel granted financial aid to the League. Cf. Nicetas, *Historia*, VII, 1, 261. For Manuel's financial support see also Lamma, *op. cit.*, II, 154-59.
   The cooperation between Manuel and Alexander III ended only ten years later, after the victory of the Lombard League over the armies of Barbarossa at Legnano (1176). Barbarossa gave up his efforts for the domination of Italy and negotiations started between him and Alexander III at Anagni. In the preliminary discussions Alexander still considered Manuel as his ally, whom he intended to include in the peace treaty, one year later, however, the treaty concluded in 1177 at Venice does not mention the Byzantine Emperor. Cf. Chalandon, *Jean Comnène et Manuel Comnène*, II, 567; Pacaut, *Alexandre III*, pp. 124-125.

9. The Hungarian custom of succession was well known in Byzantium and the Emperors often granted asylum to exiled Hungarian pretenders; cf. Cinnamus, *Historia*, I, 4, 9, and V, 1, 203.

10. Marczali, *History of Hungary*, pp. 294-295; Chalandon, *Jean Comnène et Manuel Comnène*, II, 470-471.

11. Chalandon, *Jean Comnène et Manuel Comnène*, II, 523-524.

12. Henry of Mügeln, *Chronicon*, 53, ed. E. Szentpétery, *Scriptores Rerum Hungaricarum* (Budapest, 1937), II.

13. Cinnamus, *Historia*, V, 5, 211; Nicetas, *Historia*, IV, 1, 166; cf. Chalandon, *Jean Comnène et Manuel Comnène*, II, 472-474. There is divergence concerning the time of Manuel's intervention in Hungary following Géza's death. Chalandon follows the information of the *Chronicon Pictum* which puts the death of Géza II and the subsequent throne dispute in the year 1161. Cinnamus and Nicetas are not specific about the date of Manuel's intervention. It is, however, known that Manuel in 1161 was still deeply involved in the affairs of the East and came to terms with Kilidj Arslan only toward the end of 1161. Furthermore, he celebrated his second marriage in December, 1161 and shortly after received the visit of Kilidj Arslan in Constantinople. All these facts preclude the possibility that Manuel could have spent several months during 1161 in the Balkans, waiting for the solution of the Hungarian succession. The more recent Hungarian and some foreign historians therefore lean to the view that Manuel's intervention occurred in 1162. Cf. Hóman-Szekfü, *History of Hungary* (in Hungarian), I, 381-82.; Marczali, *op. cit.*, pp. 293, 295; Ohnsorge, *op. cit.*, p. 450. Concerning Manuel's second marriage and the agreement with Kilidj Arslan, see Chalandon, *Jean Comnène et Manuel Comnène*, pp. 462, 474, 523.

14. Cinnamus, *Historia*, V, 1, 203; Thuroczy, *Chronica Hungarorum*, II, 67, ed. Schwandtner, *Scriptores Rerum Hungaricarum Veteres*, I; cf. Chalandon, *Jean Comnène et Manuel Comnène*, II, 472-473; Marczali, *op. cit.*, p. 295.

15. Thuroczy, *Chronica*, II, 68; Marczali, *History of Hungary*, p. 296; Hóman-Szekfü, *op. cit.*, I, 382.

16. Otto of Freising, *The Deeds of Frederick*, p. 335; H. Sudendorf, *Registrum oder merkwürdige Urkunden für die deutsche Geschichte* (Jena-Berlin, 1849-1854), I, 61; Marczali, *History of Hungary*, p. 298; Ohnsorge, *op. cit.*, pp. 451-452.

17. *Annales Posonienses*, ed. E. Szentpétery, *Scriptores Rerum Hungaricarum* (Budapest, 1937), I, 119-127; Mügeln, *Chronicon*, 78; Thuroczy, *Chronica Hungarorum*, II, 68.

18. Concerning the accession of Stephen Nemanja to power in Rascia there is varied information. Some sources place it in the year 1159; according to Ostrogorsky he was made grand zupan by Manuel in 1166 or 1167. The divergence probably arose because Manuel was repeatedly forced to depose and replace the disloyal zupans, among them the sons of Uros, Pervoslav, and Dessa. Stephen Nemanja, founder of the Nemanjid dynasty and forefather of the independent Serbian state, was an unwilling vassal of Manuel and repeatedly rebelled against Byzantium. After Manuel's death he was able to secure the independence of Rascia and extended his authority over Zeta as well. In 1196 he abdicated and entered the monastery of mount Athos where he died in 1198 or 1199. Cf. Chalandon, *Jean Comnène et Manuel Comnène*, II, 391-98; Ostrogorsky, *op. cit.*, pp. 345, 354; K. Jirecek,

Geschichte der Serben (Gotha, 1911-18), I, 264; F. Dvornik, *The Slavs in European History and Civilization* (New Brunswick, 1962), pp. 89-94.

19. Cinnamus, *Historia,* V, 5, 212-213; Chalandon, *Jean Comnène et Manuel Comnène,* II, 393, 475.

20. Cinnamus, *Historia,* V, 5, 215; Marczali, *History of Hungary,* p. 298; Chalandon, *Jean Comnène et Manuel Comnène,* II, 475-476.

21. Cf. Gy. Moravcsik, "Pour une alliance byzantino-hongroise," *Byzantion,* VIII (1933), 557; Hóman-Szekfü, *History of Hungary,* I, 383; Marczali, *History of Hungary,* pp. 298-299; Chalandon, *Jean Comnène et Manuel Comnène,* II, 476.

22. F. Dölger, "Ungarn in der byzantinischen Reichspolitik," *Archivum Europae Centro-Orientalis,* VIII, 3-4 (Budapest-Leipzig, 1942), 335-36.

23. Cinnamus, *Historia,* V, 6, 215; Nicetas, *Historia,* IV, 1, 167; Chalandon, *Jean Comnène et Manuel Comnène,* II, 476.

24. Nicetas, *Historia,* III, 1, 147, IV, 4, 179; Chalandon, *Jean Comnène et Manuel Comnène,* I, 223, II, 486.

25. This approved the imperial declaration concerning the council's decisions in the question of the nature of the Savior. Cf. Nicetas Choniates, *Ex Libris Thesauri Orthodoxae Fidei,* XXV, 3, 1, ed. Migne, *Patrologia Graeca,* CXL, 252; Chalandon, *Jean Comnène et Manuel Comnène,* II, 649.

26. Cinnamus, *Historia,* V, 6, 217-18; Nicetas, *Historia,* IV, 1, 167; Moravcsik, *op. cit.,* p. 557.

27. Cinnamus, *Historia,* V, 5, 215, V, 6, 217.

28. *Ibid.,* V, 5, 215.

29. *Ibid.,* V, 6, 216. The inadequacy of the information results from the fact that Stephen IV made several attempts to gain the throne and the sources do not distinguish them clearly. Cf. Chalandon, *Jean Comnène et Manuel Comnène,* II, 476-83.

30. Cinnamus, *Historia,* V, 6, 217-18; Petrikon is perhaps identical with present-day Petrovaradin.

31. *Ibid.,* V, 12, 235.

32. Vincent of Prague, *Annales,* ed. W. Wattenbach, *Monumenta Germaniae Historica Scriptores,* XVII, 681-682.

33. Cinnamus, *Historia,* V, 8, 223.

34. Vincent of Prague, *loc. cit.*

35. Cinnamus, *Historia,* V, 8, 224.

36. *Ibid.,* V, 8, 226-227.

37. *Ibid.,* V, 10, 231.

38. *Ibid.,* V, 12, 236.

39. Chalandon, *Jean Comnène et Manuel Comnène,* II, 482.

40. Vincent of Prague, *Annales,* XVII, 682.

41. Cinnamus, *Historia,* V, 9, 231, V, 12, 237.

42. Thuroczy, *Chronica Hungarorum,* II, 68; Nicetas, *Historia,* IV, 1, 167; Chalandon, *Jean Comnène et Manuel Comnène,* II, 483; Marczali, *History of Hungary,* p. 300.

43. Cinnamus, *Historia,* V, 13-16, 240-245.

44. *Ibid.,* V, 16-17, 247-249.

45. Nicetas, *Historia,* IV, 4, 179; Chalandon, *Jean Comnène et Manuel Comnène,* II, 486.

46. Nicetas, *Historia,* IV, 3, 173; Cinnamus, *Historia,* VI, 2-3, 257-258.

47. Cinnamus, *Historia*, VI, 4, 260-263; cf. Chalandon, *Jean Comnène et Manuel Comnène*, II, 487.

48. Nicholas, count of Arbe, son of the Doge Michele Vitali, married a Hungarian princess, probably a sister of Stephen III, who arrived from Hungary with a special escort in 1166. The marriage took place in Venice in 1167. Cf. A. Dandolo, *Chronicon*, ed. Muratori, *Rerum Italicarum Scriptores* (Milan, 1728), XII, 292; Marczali, *History of Hungary*, p. 301; Chalandon, *Jean Comnène et Manuel Comnène*, II, 585.

49. Cinnamus, *Historia*, VI, 4, 261; Ohnsorge, *op. cit.*, p. 452.

50. Otto of Freising, *The Deeds of Frederick*, p. 336; H. Pelzer, *Friedrichs I Politik gegen Dänemark, Polen und Ungarn* (Münster, 1906), pp. 17ff.

51. Cinnamus, *Historia*, VI, 5, 263-265; Chalandon, *Jean Comnène et Manuel Comnène*, II, 488.

52. Cinnamus, *Historia*, VI, 7, 270; Nicetas, *Historia*, V, 1, 196-197; cf. Marczali, *History of Hungary*, p. 301.

53. Nicetas, *Historia*, V, 2, 200.

54. *Ibid.*, V, 3, 202-203; Marczali, *History of Hungary*, p. 302.

55. Cinnamus, *Historia*, VI, 7, 271-272.

56. *Ibid.*, VI, 7, 273; Nicetas, *Historia*, V, 3, 204.

57. In Spalato between 1171 and 1180 and in Ragusa in 1166 and 1178 the official documents are dated after the years of Manuel's reign. In the conflict which developed in 1171 between Venice and the Byzantine Empire, the Venetians attacked the Dalmatian cities which were held by the Byzantines. According to Nicetas Dalmatian cities provided ships for the Byzantine fleet. Cf. Lucius, *De regno Dalmatiae et Croatiae*, ed. Schwandtner, *Scriptores Rerum Hungaricarum Veteres*, III, 328, 330; Nicetas, *Historia*, V, 9, 224; Chalandon, *Jean Comnène et Manuel Comnène*, II, 490-491, 589. Novak, *op. cit.*, I, 116-17.

58. Cinnamus, *Historia*, VI, 11, 287; Nicetas, *Historia*, V, 8, 220-221.

59. After the dissolution of Béla's engagement, negotiations were conducted between Byzantium and the court of Palermo for a marriage of Maria with William II, the king of Sicily. Between 1170 and 1172 Manuel, in a last attempt to improve relations with Germany, entered into negotiations for a possible marriage of Maria with Barbarossa's son Henry. Finally Maria was married to Renier of Monferrat, the son of Barbarossa's chief opponent in northern Italy. Cf. Chalandon, *Jean Comnène et Manuel Comnène*, II, 570, 596, 600.

60. Nicetas, *Historia*, V, 8, 220-221; Chalandon, *Jean Comnène et Manuel Comnène*, I, 215, II, 491; Moravcsik, "Pour une alliance . . . ," *Byzantion*, VIII (1933), 557.

61. Arnold of Lübeck, *Chronica Slavorum*, ed. Lappenberg, *Monumenta Germaniae Historica Scriptores*, XXI, 117; cf. Chalandon, *Jean Comnène et Manuel Comnène*, II, 491-492; B. Hóman, *A magyar középkor története* ("History of the Hungarian Middle Ages"), in Hungarian (Budapest, 1938), p. 362.

62. Cinnamus, *Historia*, VI, 11, 286-87; Nicetas, *Historia*, V, 8, 221.

63. Marczali, *History of Hungary*, p. 313; Hóman, *loc. cit.*

64. Marczali, *loc. cit.*; Ohnsorge, *op. cit.*, p. 453; Hóman, *op. cit.*, p. 363.

65. Béla's wife was daughter of Constance of Antioch from her second marriage with Reginald of Châtillon, and had family connections in France.

66. Cinnamus, *Historia*, VII, 3, 299; Fejér, *Codex Diplomaticus Hungariae*, II, 201-202; cf. Marczali, *History of Hungary*, pp. 313-314; Chalandon, *Jean Comnène et Manuel Comnène*, II, 492.

CHAPTER SIX

1. Chalandon, *Histoire de la domination normande en Italie et en Sicile*, II, 299-300.
2. Chalandon, *Jean Comnène et Manuel Comnène*, II, 562-563; Lamma, *Comneni e Staufer*, II, 88-102, 195-205; Pacaut, *Alexandre III*, pp. 233-234.
3. Chalandon, *Jean Comnène et Manuel Comnène*, II, 567.
4. Romuald of Salerno, *Chronicon*, ed. Arndt, *Monumenta Germaniae Historica Scriptores*, XIX, 439; Dandolo, *Chronicon*, ed. Muratori, *Rerum Italicarum Scriptores*, XII, 289. The sources are somewhat obscure about the time of the offer. Chalandon's view, that there were two such proposals for the marriage between Maria and William, one already in 1166, seems not too convincing because of Maria's engagement with Béla-Alexius, which in 1166 was still in effect. Cf. Chalandon, *Histoire de la domination normande*, II, 358-359, 368, 371.
5. Romuald of Salerno, *loc. cit.*; Chalandon, *Histoire de la domination normande*, II, 372.
6. Arnold of Lübeck, *Chronica Slavorum*, XXI, 117; Chalandon, *Jean Comnène et Manuel Comnène*, II, 596; Ohnsorge, *op. cit.*, p. 475; Lamma, *op. cit.*, II, 230-233.
7. Cf. Ohnsorge, *op. cit.*, pp. 477-478.
8. Romuald of Salerno, *Chronicon*, XIX, 441; Nicetas, *Historia*, VII, 1, 262; cf. Chalandon, *Jean Comnène et Manuel Comnène*, II, 597.
9. *Ibid.*, II, 599.
10. Ohnsorge, *op. cit.*, p. 480.
11. See above chapter V, p. 107.
12. Cinnamus, *Historia*, VI, 10, 282; Nicetas, *Historia*, V, 9, 223.
13. Cinnamus, *loc. cit.*; Nicetas, *loc. cit.*; Lamma, *op. cit.*, II, 208-215.
14. Lamma, *op. cit.*, II, 225-227; Chalandon, *Jean Comnène et Manuel Comnène*, II, 589-591.
15. According to Nicetas, Manuel negotiated a new agreement with the Venetians, renewing their privileges. Dandolo contradicts Nicetas' information attributing the agreement to Andronicus who followed Manuel on the Byzantine throne in 1183. Cf. Nicetas, *Historia*, V, 9, 225; Dandolo, *Chronicon*, ed. Muratori, *Rerum Italicarum Scriptores*, XII, 309; Chalandon, *Jean Comnène et Manuel Comnène*, II, 592; Lamma, *op. cit.*, II, 226.
16. *Ibid.*, II, 286; Fliche-Martin, *op. cit.*, IX, Part 2, 152-153; Chalandon, *Jean Comnène et Manuel Comnène*, II, 598.
17. Chalandon, *Jean Comnène et Manuel Comnène*, II, 495, 501; Bréhier, *Vie et mort de Byzance*, pp. 339, 341; Lamma, *op. cit.*, II, 254.
18. Vasiliev, *History of the Byzantine Empire*, II, 428.
19. A detailed contemporary report about the battle is provided by Nicetas, *Historia*, VI, 2, 231-234, 236; cf. Chalandon, *Jean Comnène et Manuel Comnène*, II, 506-512; Lamma, *op. cit.*, II, 278-283.
20. Nicetas, *Historia*, VI, 4, 240-242; Chalandon, *loc. cit.*

21. Nicetas, *Historia*, VI, 6, 248.

22. Cf. Chalandon, *Jean Comnène et Manuel Comnène*, II, 512.

23. Nicetas, *Historia*, VII, 1, 261.

24. Lamma, *op. cit.*, II, 301-302. The marriage of Maria and Renier of Montferrat ended in a disaster for both. After Manuel's death the couple remained in Constantinople and they were instrumental in fomenting a revolt aganist the regency of Manuel's widow and the succession of young Alexius II. This ultimately led to the intervention of Manuel's cousin Andronicus, who eliminated all possible rivals and seized power. Maria and Renier were poisoned, the Empress Marie of Antioch and Alexius II were strangled at Andronicus' order. Cf. Bréhier, *op. cit.*, pp. 343-346.

25. Jaffe, *Regesta*, No. 11883, 11894; Chalandon, *Jean Comnène et Manuel Comnène*, II, 567; Ch. Diehl, *Byzantine Empresses*, trans. H. Bell and Th. Kerpely (New York, 1963), p. 245.

26. Chalandon, *Jean Comnène et Manuel Comnène*, II, 605; Diehl, *Byzantine Empresses*, pp. 246-47.

27. Nicetas, *Historia*, VII, 7, 287.

28. Ostrogorsky, *op. cit.*, pp. 355-62; Bréhier, *op. cit.*, pp. 345-355.

29. Marczali, *History of Hungary*, p. 314; Novak, *op. cit.*, p. 118.

30. Nicetas, *Historia, Imperium Alexii Porphyrogeniti* 17, 347; cf. Moravcsik, "Pour une alliance . . . ," *Byzantion*, VIII (1933), 561.

31. Ostrogorsky, *op. cit.*, p. 351-352; *Cambridge Medieval History*, IV, 382.

32. Hóman, *History of the Hungarian Middle Ages*, p. 365; Ostrogorsky, *op. cit.*, p. 354.

33. Moravcsik, *op. cit.*, p. 562; Hóman, *loc. cit.*

34. Nicetas, *Historia Imperium Isaacii Angeli*, I, 4, 481.

35. Hóman, *History of the Hungarian Middle Ages*, p. 365; Novak, *op. cit.*, I, 118.

36. Marczali, *History of Hungary*, pp. 318, 330, 336; Hóman, *History of the Hungarian Middle Ages*, p. 370; Moravcsik, *op. cit.*, p. 566.

37. Nicetas, *Historia. De imperio Isaacii Angeli*, III, 8, 588-595; Moravcsik, *op. cit.*, p. 567; Ostrogorsky, *op. cit.*, p. 362.

CONCLUSION

1. Chalandon, *Jean Comnène et Manuel Comnène*, II, 607; Vasiliev, *History of the Byzantine Empire*, II, 431; Ostrogorsky, *op. cit.*, pp. 341-348.

2. Nicetas, *Historia*, VII, 1, 260-261.

Bibliography*

I

PRIMARY SOURCES

1. *Byzantine authors*—For the beginning of the period of the Com-neni, the accession of Alexius I Comnenus, and for the period of the First Crusade an important source was provided by Alexius' daughter, ANNA COMNENA, in her epic the *Alexiad*.

Anna, as a child, was engaged to Constantine Ducas and together with her fiancé was proclaimed presumptive heir to the throne by her father. Following the birth of Alexius' son John, however, Anna was deprived of the right of succession. After the death of Constantine Ducas she married Nicephorus Bryennius and lost all hope of ever obtaining the imperial crown. These circumstances explain Anna's bitter enmity against John Comnenus, a hatred which prompted her to form secret plots against her own brother. Her actions remained unsuccessful and Anna, fallen into disgrace, lived for thirty years in the seclusion of a convent.

Under the epic title, Anna Comnena dedicated her work to the history of her father's achievements, and obviously tried to place the career of Alexius Comnenus in the best light while deliberately obscur-ing the person of her brother. Her attitude toward the western Cru-saders is also strongly biased. In spite of these deficiencies the *Alexiad*, based on personal and contemporary information, has signal historic and literary value.

For the period of the Comneni two Byzantine historians were of particular interest. The works of both can be regarded as continua-tions of Anna Comnena's work.

---

* Alphabetical listing of sources with full bibliographical information is given in section II; see p. **154**

JOANNES CINNAMUS wrote a history of the reigns of John II and Manuel Comnenus under the title *Historia*, which is preserved in an abridged manuscript in the Vatican Library.

Very little is known about the author's life. He was contemporary to Manuel Comnenus and probably held the post of secretary (*grammatikos*) in the imperial military administration. According to his own statement he lived at court and accompanied the emperor on various campaigns in Asia Minor and Europe.*

The work starts with the reign of John Comnenus, but its major interest lies in the section dealing with the events of Manuel's reign. Here the author had been an eyewitness to a number of developments. His account is based in part on first-hand information and on original documents, whose authenticity, however, sometimes seems to be doubtful. The central figure of the narrative is Manuel and Cinnamus presents his hero idealized. He also follows the official political line of the court by defending the universalistic concepts of the Byzantine Empire, and he shares the general Greek antagonism towards the western crusaders.

Nevertheless, Cinnamus' work deserves attention because of his efforts to gather accurate information. Despite personal bias, he does not seem consciously to alter the facts which he reports. Cinnamus' work has particular interest from the point of view of Byzantine-Hungarian relations. He reports Manuel's various campaigns against Hungary in such detail that his account often evokes the impression of personal experience.

The most important historian of the Comnenian period is NICETAS ACOMINATUS, called also CHONIATES after the name of his native city, Chonae in Phrygia. He was born around the middle of the twelfth century, and entered the imperial civil service probably during the last years of Manuel's reign. Here he attained high positions under the Emperor Isaac Angelus, and after the sack of Constantinople by the Fourth Crusade, he fled to the court of the Emperor Theodore Lascaris, where he lived some ten more years completing his great history. He probably died between 1210 and 1220 at Nicaea.

Nicetas' work, the *History*, covers a period of almost ninety years from the accession of John Comnenus to the first years of the Latin empire (1118-1206).

The first part of the work deals with the reign of John Comnenus, and here Nicetas' information is often incomplete. On the relations

---

* Cinnamus, *Historia,* I, 1, 5.

between Byzantium and Hungary and on affairs in the Balkans more accurate and valuable information is provided in the seven books concerning the reign of Manuel Comnenus. These books include discussions of the Second Crusade, the Norman attack on Corfù, Corinth, and the Peloponnesus, and Manuel's preparations for a counter-move against Roger II in 1149. There follows a description of the Serbian revolt and a detailed narrative of Manuel's Serbian and Hungarian campaigns. Nicetas also enters into a discussion of the succession disputes in Hungary, the connections of the Byzantine court with the various pretenders, Manuel's agreement with Stephen III, his adoption of Béla, the engagement of Manuel's daughter to Béla, and the proclamation of Béla as heir to the Byzantine throne.

A coordinated review of these scattered parts of Nicetas' narrative reveals that Manuel's attention following the first Serbian revolt in 1149 had been focused chiefly on the Balkans and Hungary. This supports the contention that Manuel's failure to concentrate all efforts on his western plans and to win control of Italy was connected with his involvement in Hungarian affairs.

As a historian, Nicetas on the whole is fair and unprejudiced, although he is not free from the resentment which most Byzantines felt toward the Latins. In contrast to Cinnamus, Nicetas is more impartial in his judgment about Manuel's person and policies, not hesitating to show the costs and the unfavorable consequences of Manuel's ambitious foreign policy. In the seventh book about Manuel, however, which was probably written after the collapse of 1204, Nicetas reversed his opinion about the *basileus* and recognized the positive values of Manuel's foreign political conceptions.

2. *Hungarian sources*—In the eleventh century, the first century of the medieval Christian kingdom of Hungary, the only literate class in Hungary consisted almost entirely of foreigners—missionaries and churchmen who were organizing the new religion. Thus the first historical accounts of this period in Hungary might have been written by Italians or Germans.

The eleventh century in Hungary, following the conversion of her first king, Stephen, and his marriage to the Bavarian princess, Gisella, was in any event a period of strong foreign cultural influence, enhanced by the continuous presence of foreigners at the royal court. It is interesting to note in this connection that, following St. Stephen, all subsequent rulers of the Arpád family invariably intermarried with foreign ruling families. The history of this national dynasty of Hungary does not show a single Hungarian-born queen.

The earliest Hungarian medieval source which survives, the *Gesta Hungarorum*, probably dates back to the late twelfth century. It is commonly known as the *Chronicle of Anonymus* because the identity of its author, probably a royal notary at the court of Béla III, is unknown, and is, perhaps, the most famous but also the least reliable of all Hungarian chronicles. It deals with the origin and the first two centuries of the Hungarian nation in Europe, including romanticized stories of the first Hungarian contacts with Byzantium in the form of marauding expeditions.

Modern Hungarian historiography speculates about the existence of an earlier *Gesta Hungarorum*, composed possibly between 1080 and 1090. The original of this hypothetical work is supposed to have been lost, though it may have served as source for Anonymus' chronicle, and even more for two later medieval historians, Simeon of Kézai and Marc of Kált. This belief is supported by the almost identical presentation of certain earlier events in the works of these later historians.*

SIMEON OF KEZAI in his *Gesta Hungarorum* gives the history of the Hungarians from the earliest times to his own day, which probably coincides with the reign of King Ladislas IV (1272-1290).

The first part of the work, the so-called "Hun Chronicle," deals with the exploits of Attila and the Huns, from whom Kézai wants to trace the origin of the Magyar nation. The chronicle is relatively complete up to the time of St. Stephen and the period immediately succeeding. After that, notably for the period of Byzantine-Hungarian relations under the Comneni, the *Gesta* is more or less only an annotated list of the kings of Hungary up to the reign of Ladislas IV, who again receives enthusiastic treatment.

Two other narrative chronicles took over practically verbatim all the material of Kézai's work, carrying on the story to a later date.

The *Chronicon Budense* was probably composed around 1330 and is a compilation from various sources, among them Kézai's chronicle. The compilation was done by different persons, and from the early twelfth century on it is rather rough and superficial, furnishing very little for the Comnenian period. The *Chronicon Budense* also appeared in printed form in 1473, dedicated by the printer to King Mathias Corvinus. It was the first printed book in Hungary.

The *Chronicon Pictum*, formerly known as *Chronicon Pictum*

---

* C. A. Macartney, *The Medieval Hungarian Historians* (Cambridge, 1953), pp. 15-24.

Vindobonense, received its name from a magnificent illuminated codex which formerly was in Vienna and now is kept in Budapest. The codex was copied between 1374 and 1376 from an original dating back to 1358. Its author, MARC DE KALT, was canon of the bishopric of Székesfehérvár, the ancient capital and burial place of the Arpád dynasty.

The chronicle inserts the story transmitted by Kézai and the *Chronicon Budense,* but for the later period, notably from the end of the eleventh century on, it seems to utilize other sources, both Hungarian and Russian. It provides valuable information, although chronologically sometimes confused, about the reign of Coloman and his conflict with Almos, the affair of Boris, and the Byzantine-Hungarian conflict under Stephen III.

The text of the *Chronicon Pictum,* taken over verbatim, forms the first three books of the *Chronica Hungarorum* of JOANNES THUROCZY, published in printed form in 1488 at Buda, Mathias Corvinus' capital.

The author was *protonotarius,* a high ranking official of the judicial administration, under Mathias Corvinus. He was already a renaissance historian who produced valuable work for his own period. He did not, however, contribute anything new for the period of the Comneni and the Arpáds, simply taking over the bulk of the *Chronicon Budense* and the *Chronicon Pictum* and eventually increasing it with some elements borrowed from classical models.

3. *Western sources*—Among the western primary sources of the Comnenian period, the works of Odo of Deuil and Otto of Freising are of signal importance, although for Hungarian affairs their information is much more limited than that of the Byzantine or Hungarian sources.

ODO OF DEUIL, royal chaplain at the court of Louis VII and later abbot of St. Denis, accompanied Louis VII during the Second Crusade and described the journey of the French army in his work, *De profectione Ludovici VII in orientem.*

As a source of information, not only for the crusade itself, but also for the countries and places which the French army traversed, Odo's work is quite outstanding. He presents the events lucidly and correctly from the geographical point of view, and his statements are based on his own observations or on first hand information. A few brief paragraphs of Odo's work mention the passage of the German emperor across Hungary, and also give an interesting topographical description of the part of Hungary which the French crossed. Another part of the same book describes the encounter of Louis VII and Géza II, the appearance of the pretender Boris in the French camp, and Géza's unsuccessful plea for Boris' extradition.

The other important western source concerning the Comnenian period is OTTO OF FREISING'S work, the *Gesta Friderici I imperatoris*, which covers the period from 1152 to 1160. The author, a Cistercian monk, later bishop of Freising, earned his reputation as an outstanding historian-philosopher of the twelfth century by his major work, *De duabus civitatibus* ("The Two Cities"), a philosophical interpretation in eight books of world history to 1146.

As half-brother of Emperor Conrad III, Otto participated in the Second Crusade. He played a considerable political role as uncle of Emperor Frederick Barbarossa. He was well informed about the underlying causes of certain events and his information is especially valuable concerning the contacts between Conrad III and John Comnenus, as well as the long and difficult negotiations between Barbarossa and Manuel.

The affairs of Hungary are also discussed by Otto. He describes Boris' attempt to seize the Hungarian throne with German help and the battle on the Fischa between King Géza II and Henry of Babenberg. Similarly, Otto reports on Barbarossa's plan to invade Hungary and the Diet of Regensburg in 1152 which dwarfed Barbarossa's plan.

SECONDARY SOURCES

Among the principal secondary sources concerning the period of the Comneni the most important work is a great monograph in two parts (three volumes) by FERDINAND CHALANDON, *Les Comnène. Etudes sur l'Empire Byzantin au XIe et au XIIe siècles,* first published in Paris between 1900 and 1912. The first part is an essay about the reign of Alexius I Comnenus (*Essai sur le règne d'Alexis Ier Comnène*). The second part in two volumes deals with the political and social aspects of the Byzantine Empire under John II and Manuel Comnenus (*Jean Comnène et Manuel Comnène*).

Chalandon's work recently has been partly superseded by an important work in Italian by PAOLO LAMMA in two volumes under the title *Comneni e Staufer. Ricerche sui rapporti fra Bisanzio e l'Occidente nel secolo XII*, published in Rome by the Istituto Storico Italiano per il Medio Evo in 1957. Lamma's work is particularly valuable for the excellent presentation of Manuel's western political concepts, the problem of southern Italy, and the rivalry between the two empires, both with universalistic tendencies.

Among works of a general character which add valuable information for the study of the Comnenian period are: A. A. Vasiliev's *History of the Byzantine Empire* (1958), G. Ostrogorsky's *History of the Byzantine State* (1957), and L. Bréhier's *Le Monde byzantin. Vie et mort de Byzance* (1947).

For the papal schism of the twelfth century, the pontificate of Alexander III and his relations with Frederick Barbarossa and with Manuel, the ninth volume of the series *Histoire de l'Eglise* by A. Fliche and V. Martin (1953) provides many important details.

The new (1966) edition of volume IV of *The Cambridge Medieval History*, in chapter XII by M. Dinic, discusses extensively the Balkan relations of the Byzantine Empire from 1018 till the Turkish conquest of the Balkans. The interest is focused, however, on the decline of Byzantine influence in the Balkans, on the rise of Serbian independence, and the formation of the second Bulgarian empire, with little attention given to the Comnenian period.

In chapter XIII of the same volume, Gy. Moravcsik discusses the cultural, ecclesiastical, and diplomatic ties between Byzantium and Hungary from the earliest contacts till the end of the Arpád dynasty (1301). A brief section is devoted to Manuel's campaigns on the Danube frontier and his interventionist policy towards Hungary as an element in a greater European political scheme. The connections between his military and diplomatic moves in the Balkans and his political objectives in Italy are not revealed.

The Hungarian secondary sources deal with relations between Hungary and the Byzantine Empire mainly from two points of view. Since the Byzantine Empire was in contact with the Hungarians even before they settled down permanently in their present land, Byzantine historians and diplomats provide valuable information about the earliest history of the Hungarian nation. Because of this, Byzantine historical sources have been investigated by several Hungarian historians. Here belongs the work of Gy. Moravcsik, *Byzantinoturcica. Die Byzantinischen Quellen der Geschichte der Türkvölker* (1942), as well as M. Gyóni's work, *Ungarn und das Ungartum im Spiegel der Byzantinischen Quellen* (1938).

The major Hungarian general historical works on the other hand, like H. Marczali's *History of Hungary in the age of the Árpáds* (1896, in Hungarian), the standard *History of Hungary* (1938, in Hungarian) by B. Homan and J. Szekfü, or the short monograph by

154 BYZANTIUM AND THE DANUBE FRONTIER

L. Thalloczy, *Béla III and the Hungarian kingdom* (1900, in Hungarian) discuss the relations between the Byzantine Empire and medieval Hungary strictly from the Hungarian point of view. Gy. Moravcsik, in his work *Byzantium and the Hungarians* (1953, in Hungarian), investigates Byzantine interference in the succession disputes within the Arpád dynasty and the armed conflicts which resulted from this interference. He focuses his interest primarily on the impact of these conflicts on Hungarian developments, and attributes particular importance to the idea and possibility of a personal union between Byzantium and Hungary, a conception which, however, failed to materialize.

I I

PRIMARY SOURCES

Anna Comnena. *Alexiade*. French trans. B. Leib. 3 vols. Paris, 1937-45.
———. *The Alexiad*. English trans. E. Dawes. London, 1928.
———. *The Alexiad*. Ed. Reifferscheid. 2 vols. Leipzig, 1884.
Anonymus, Belae regis notarius. *De gestis Hungarorum*. Ed J. Schwandtner. *Scriptores Rerum Hungaricarum Veteres,* I. Vienna, 1746-48.
Chronicon Budense (Chronica Hungarorum). Ed. V. Fraknoi. Budapest, 1900.
Chronicon Pictum Marci de Kalt (Chronicon Pictum Vindobonense). Ed. and Hungarian trans. L. Geréb. Budapest, 1959.
Chronicon Posoniense. Ed. Endlicher. *Rerum Hungaricarum Monumenta Arpadiana*. Sangalli, 1849.
Cinnamus, Joannes. *Historia*. Ed. J. P. Migne. *Patrologia Graeca,* CXXXIII. Paris, 1864.
Dandolo, Andrea. *Chronicon Venetum*. Ed. L. A. Muratori. *Rerum Italicarum Scriptores*, XII. Milan, 1728.
Diocleas Presbyter. *Regnum Slavorum* (Ljetopis Popa Dukljanina). Ed. and Croatian trans. V. Mosin. Zagreb, 1950.
———. *Chronicon*, in J. Lucius, *De regno Dalmatiae (1666)*. Ed. J. Schwandtner. *Scriptores Rerum Hungaricarum Veteres*. III. Vienna, 1746-48.
Kézai, Simeon de. *Chronicon*. Ed. J. Schwandtner. *Scriptores Rerum Hungaricarum Veteres*, I. Vienna, 1746-48.

Lucius, Joannes. *De regno Dalmatiae et Croatiae libri sex.* Ed. J. Schwandtner. *Scriptores Rerum Hungaricarum Veteres,* III. Vienna, 1746-48.

Monumenta Serbica spectantia historiam Serbiae, Bosniae et Ragusii. Ed. F. Miklosich. Vienna, 1859.

Mügeln, Henricus. *Chronicon.* Ed. Emeric Szentpétery. *Scriptores Rerum Hungaricarum tempore ducum regumque stirpis Arpadianae gestarum,* II. Budapest, 1937.

Nicetas Choniates. *Historia.* Ed. J. P. Migne. *Patrologia Graeca,* CXXXIX. Paris, 1864.

Odo de Deuil. *De profectione Ludovici VII in orientem.* Ed. and trans. Virginia G. Berry. New York, 1948.

Otto of Freising. *Chronicon. Historia de duabus civitatibus.* Ed. R. Wilmans. *Monumenta Germaniae Historica Scriptores,* XX. Hannover, 1868.

————. *Gesta Frederici Imperatoris* ("The Deeds of Frederick Barbarossa and his Continuator, Rahewin"). Ed. and trans. Charles Mierow. New York, 1953.

Psellus, Michael. *Chronographia.* Ed. and trans. E. R. A. Sewter. New Haven, 1953.

Romuald of Salerno. *Chronicon.* Ed. Arndt. *Monumenta Germaniae Historica Scriptores.* XIX. Hannover, 1868.

Scylitzes, Joannes. *Historia.* Ed. J. P. Migne. *Patrologia Graeca,* CXXII. Paris, 1864.

The Russian Primary Chronicle. Laurentian Text. Ed. and trans. S. H. Cross and O. P. Sherbowitz-Wetzor. Cambridge, 1953.

Thuroczy, Joannes. *Chronica Hungarorum.* Ed. J. Schwandtner. *Scriptores Rerum Hungaricarum Veteres,* I. Vienna, 1746-48.

Vincent of Prague. *Annales.* Ed. W. Wattenbach. *Monumenta Germaniae Historica Scriptores.* XVII.

William of Tyre. *A History of Deeds Done Beyond The Sea.* Trans. and annot. E. A. Babcock and A. Ch. Krey. New York, 1943.

————. *Historia rerum in partibus transmarinis gestarum. Recueil des historiens des croisades. Historiens occidentaux.* I-II. Paris, 1869-81.

SECONDARY SOURCES

Barraclough, Geoffrey. *History in a Changing World.* Oxford, 1956.
————. *The Origins of Modern Germany.* New York, 1963.

Baynes, Norman. *The Byzantine Empire*. London, 1949.
———— and Moss, H. St. L. B. *Byzantium*. Oxford, 1948.
Bernhardi, Wilhelm. *Konrad III*. Leipzig, 1883.
Berry, Virginia G. "The Second Crusade," *A History of the Cru-sades*. Ed. K. Setton and M. W. Baldwin. Philadelphia, 1955.
Bratianu, G. J. "Byzance et la Hongrie," *Revue historique du sud-est européen*, XXII (1945), 147 ff.
Bréhier, Louis. *Le monde byzantin. Vie et mort de Byzance*. Paris, 1947.
Buckler, Georgiana. *Anna Comnena: A Study*. Oxford, 1929.
Buechler, Samuel. *Ungarn während und nach der Kreuzzugsperiode*. New York, 1909.
Bury, J. B. *A History of the Eastern Roman Empire*. London, 1912.
Cambridge Medieval History, Vols. IV-V. Cambridge, 1927-1966.
Caspar, E. *Roger II (1101-1154) und die Gründung der norman-nisch-sizilischen Monarchie*. Innsbruck, 1904.
Chalandon, Ferdinand. *Histoire de la domination normande en Italie et en Sicile*. 2 vols. Paris, 1907.
————. *Essai sur le règne d'Alexis Ier Comnène, 1081-1118*. Paris, 1900.
————. *Les Comnène. Jean II Comnène et Manuel I Comnène*. 2 vols. Paris, 1912.
Charanis, Peter. "Byzantium, the West, and the Origin of the First Crusade," *Byzantion*, XIX (1949).
Cognasso, Francesco. *Partiti politici e lotte dinastiche in Bisanzio alla morte di Manuele Comneno*. Torino, 1912.
Curtis, E. *Roger of Sicily and the Normans in Lower Italy. 1016-1154*. New York-London, 1912.
Deér, Joseph. *Die Anfänge der ungarisch-kroatischen Staatsgemein-schaft*. ("Etudes sur l'Europe centro-orientale," Vol. IV.) Budapest, 1936.
Diehl, Charles. *Byzance: grandeur et décadence*. Paris, 1919.
————. *Byzantine Empresses*. Trans. H. Bell and Th. Kerpely. New York, 1963.
————. *Figures byzantines*. 2 vols. Paris, 1909.
————. *History of the Byzantine Empire*. Trans. G. B. Ives. Princeton, 1925.
————. *La société byzantine à l'époque des Comnènes*. Paris, 1929.
Dölger, Franz. *Byzanz. Forschungen zur byzantinischen Geschichte, Literatur und Sprache*. ("Wissenschaftliche Forschungsberichte," ed. Karl Hönn, Vol. V). Bern, 1952.

———— (ed.). *Regesten der Kaiserurkunden des Oströmischen Reiches von 565-1453.* ("Corpus der griechischen Urkunden des Mittelalters," Reihe A.). München-Berlin, 1925.

————. "Ungarn in der byzantinischen Reichspolitik," *Archivum Europae Centro-Orientalis,* VIII, 3-4 (1942), 315-342.

Dvornik, Francis. *The Making of Central and Eastern Europe.* London, 1949.

————. *The Slavs in European History and Civilization.* New Brunswick, 1962.

————. *The Slavs: Their Early History.* Boston, 1956.

Fejér, G. (ed.). *Codex Diplomaticus Hungariae.* 2 vols. Budae, 1829.

Ferluga, J. *L'administration byzantine en Dalmatie.* (Académie Serbe des sciences. Institute d'études byzantines. Monographies, 291). Belgrade, 1957.

Fliche, Augustin et Martin, Victor (eds.). *Histoire de l'Eglise depuis les origines jusqu'à nos jours,* VIII-IX. Paris, 1947-56.

Gay, J. *L'Italie méridionale et l'Empire Byzantin depuis l'avènement de Basil Ier jusqu'à la prise de Bari par les Normands, 867-1071.* Paris, 1904.

Giesebrecht, Wilhelm. *Geschichte der deutschen Kaiserzeit.* 6 vols. Braunschweig, 1875-95.

Grafenauer, B., Perovic, D., and Sidak, J. *Historija naroda Jugoslavije* ("History of the Yugoslav Nation"). Zagreb-Beograd, 1953. In Croatian.

Grot, C. *Iz istorii Ugrii i Slavianstva v XII. vieke* ("From the History of Ugria and the Slavs in the Twelfth Century"). Warsaw, 1889. In Russian.

Guerdan, René. *Byzantium, Its Triumph and Tragedy.* Trans. D. C. B. Hartley. New York, 1957.

Gyóni, M. *Magyarország és a magyarság a bizánci források tükrében* ("Hungary and the Hungarians in the Mirror of Byzantine Sources"). Budapest, 1938. In Hungarian.

Heilig, K. J. "Ostrom und das Deutsche Reich um die Mitte des XII. Jahrhunderts," in *Kaisertum und Herzogsgewalt im Zeitalter Friedrichs I.* Ed. Theodor Meyer. ("Schriften des Reichsinstituts für ältere deutsche Geschichtskunde," No. 9). Leipzig, 1944.

Holtzmann, W. "Papst Alexander III und Ungarn," *Ungarische Jahrbücher,* VI (1926), 405 ff.

Hóman, Bálint. *A magyar középkor története* ("History of the Hungarian Middle Ages"). Budapest, 1938. In Hungarian.

———. *Geschichte des ungarischen Mittelalters.* 2 vols. Berlin, 1940.

——— and Szekfü, Gyula. *Magyar Történet* ("History of Hungary"). 5 vols. Budapest, 1938. In Hungarian.

Hussey, Joan M. *The Byzantine World.* London, 1957.

Jaffé, Philip (ed.). *Regesta Pontificum Romanorum ab condita ecclesia ad annum 1198.* Lipsiae, 1885.

Jenkins, R. J. H. *The Byzantine Empire on the Eve of the Crusades.* London, 1953.

Jirecek, Konstantin. *Geschichte der Serben.* 2 vols. Gotha, 1911-18.

Kap-Herr, Hans. *Die abendländische Politik Kaiser Manuels mit besonderer Rücksicht auf Deutschland.* Strassburg, 1881.

Kosáry, Dominic G. *A History of Hungary.* Cleveland-New York, 1941.

Kugler, Bernhard. *Neue Analekten zur .Geschichte des zweiten Kreuzzugs.* Tübingen, 1883.

Lamma, Paolo. *Comneni e Staufer.* 2 vols. Roma, 1955-57.

Laurent, V. "La Serbie entre Byzance et la Hongrie à la veille de la quatrième croisade," *Revue historique du sud-est européen,* XVIII (1941), 109-130.

Leib, Bernard. *Rome, Kiev et Byzance à la fin du XIème siècle.* Paris, 1924.

Lemerle, P. *Histoire de Byzance.* Paris, 1948.

Levchenko, M. V. *Byzance dès origines à 1453.* Paris, 1949.

Macartney, Carlile A. *Hungary: A Short History.* Chicago, 1962.

———. *The Magyars in the Ninth Century.* Cambridge, 1930.

———. *The Medieval Hungarian Historians.* Cambridge, 1953.

Marczali, Henrik. *Magyarország története az Arpádok korában* ("History of Hungary in the Age of the Arpáds"). Budapest, 1896. In Hungarian.

Mladenovich, M. *L'état serbe au moyen âge.* Paris, 1931.

Moravcsik, Gyula. *Bizánc és a Magyarság* ("Byzantium and the Hungarians"). Budapest, 1953. In Hungarian.

———. *Byzantinoturcica. Byzantinische Quellen der Geschichte der Türkvölker.* Budapest, 1943.

———. "Pour une alliance byzantino-hongroise (second moitié du XIIème siècle)," *Byzantion,* VIII (1933), 555-568.

Neumann, Karl. *Die Weltstellung des Byzantinischen Reiches vor den Kreuzzügen.* Leipzig, 1894.

———. *Griechische Geschichtsschreiber und Geschichtsquellen im zwölften Jahrhundert.* Leipzig, 1888.

Norden, Walter. *Das Papsttum und Byzanz; die Trennung der*

beiden Mächte und das Problem ihrer Wiedervereinigung bis zum Untergang des Byzantinischen Reiches. Reprint. New York, 1950 .

Novak, Grga. *Proslost Dalmacije* ("The Past of Dalmatia"). 2 vols. Zagreb, 1944. In Croatian.

Ohnsorge, Werner. *Abendland und Byzanz. Gesammelte Aufsätze zur Geschichte der byzantinisch-abendländischen Beziehungen und des Kaisertums.* Darmstadt, 1958.

―――. *Ein Beitrag zur Geschichte Manuels I von Byzanz.* ("Albert Brackman Festschrift"). Weimar, 1931.

Ostrogorsky, George. "Byzantium and the South Slavs," *Slavonic and East European Review,* XLII, 98 (December, 1963), 1-14.

―――. *History of the Byzantine State.* Trans. J. Hussey. Oxford, 1956.

Pacaut, Marcel. *Alexandre III. Etudes sur la conception du pouvoir pontifical dans sa pensée et dans son oeuvre.* Paris, 1956.

Radojcic, M. *Dva posljednja Komnena na carigradskom prijestolju* ("The Last Two Comneni on the Throne of Constantinople"). Zagreb, 1907. In Croatian.

Rambaud, A. *L'empire grec au Xème siècle. Constantin Porphyrogenète.* Paris, 1870.

Reuter, Hermann. *Geschichte Alexanders des Dritten und der Kirche seiner Zeit.* 3 vols. Leipzig, 1860-64.

Rowe, John Gordon. *The Papacy and the Greeks (1122-1153).* Reprint from "Church History," Vol. XXVIII, No. 3). 1959.

Runciman, Steven. *A History of the Crusades.* 2 vols. Cambridge, 1951-52.

―――. *Byzantine Civilization.* London, 1933.

―――. *The Eastern Schism: A Study of the Papacy and the Eastern Churches during the XIth and XIIth Centuries.* Oxford, 1955.

Schönebaum, Herbert. *Die Kenntniss der byzantinischen Geschichtsschreiber von der ältesten Geschichte der Ungarn vor der Landnahme.* Berlin, 1922.

Setton, Kenneth and Baldwin, Marshall W. *A History of the Crusades.* Vol. I: *The First Hundred Years.* Ed. M. W. Baldwin. Philadelphia, 1955.

Sinor, Denis. *History of Hungary.* New York, 1959.

Sisic, F. *Geschichte der Kroaten.* Zagreb, 1917.

Stadtmüller, Georg. *Die Geschichte Südosteuropas.* München, 1950.

Stanojevic, Stano. *Istorija srpskoga naroda u srednjum veku* ("History of the Serbian nation in the middle ages"). Beograd, 1937.

In Serbian.

———. *Vizantija i Srbi* ("Byzantium and the Serbs"). 2 vols. Novi Sad, 1903-1906. In Serbian.

Stein, E. *Studien zur Geschichte des byzantinischen Reiches.* Stuttgart, 1919.

Thallóczy, Lajos. *III. Béla és a Magyar Birodalom* ("Béla III and the Hungarian Realm"). Budapest, 1906. In Hungarian.

———. "Die ungarischen Beziehungen der Chronik des Presbyter Diocleas," *Archiv für slawische Philologie,* XX (1898), 217-220.

Vasiliev, A. A. *Byzance et les Arabes.* Bruxelles, 1935.

———. *History of the Byzantine Empire.* 2 vols. Madison, 1958.

Voinovich, Lujo. *Histoire de la Dalmatie.* Trans. D. L. Hartley. Paris, 1934.

Wenzel, Gustav (ed.). *Codex Diplomaticus Arpadianus.* 12 vols. Budapest, 1860-74.

Genealogical Tables

Genealogical Table of the Dynasty of Arpad

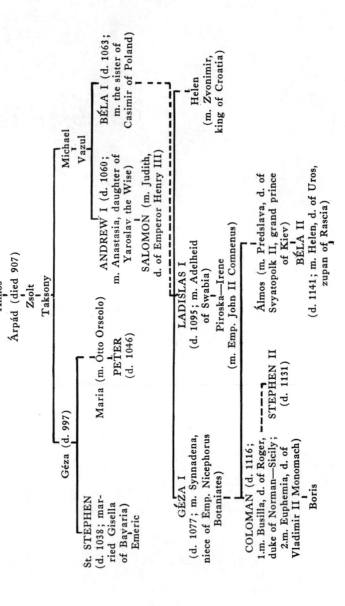

GÉZA II
(d. 1162; m. Euphrosyne,
d. of Mstislav of Kiev)

STEPHEN III
(d. 1173; m. Agnes, d. of
Henry Babenberg, duke of
Austria)

LADISLAS II
(d. 1163)

STEPHEN IV
(d. 1165; m. Maria,
d. of sebastocrator Isaac)

BÉLA III
(d. 1196; 1.m. Anne of Châtillon;
2.m. Margaret Capet, d. of Louis VII,
king of France)

EMERIC
(d. 1204;
m. Constance
of Aragon)

ANDREW II (d. 1235;
1.m. Gertrude   2.m. Yolande   3.m. Beatrix
of Meran   of Courtenay   of Este)

Margaret
(m. Emp. Isaac
Angelus)

Constance
(m. Ottokar I,
king of Bohemia)

BÉLA IV (d. 1270;
m. Maria Lascaris)

Yolande
(m. James, king
of Aragon)

Stephen
(m. Tomasina Morosini)

STEPHEN V
(d. 1272; m.
Elizabeth,
Cuman princess)

Anna (m. Ratislav,
tsar of Bulgaria)

Elizabeth
(m. Henry,
duke of
Bavaria)

ANDREW III
(d. 1301; m. Agnes of
Habsburg)

LADISLAS IV
(d. 1290; m.
Isabel of
Anjou)

Maria
(m. Charles of Anjou)

Index

Acre (city), 64

Adalbertus, envoy of Géza II, 52

Adelaide, marriage to Otto the Great, 16

Adelheid, wife of Ladislas I, king of Hungary, 26

Adriatic coast, Byzantine interest 13, 28, 33, 42, 43, 56; and R. Guiscard 35; Hohenstaufen interest 127; Hungarian expansion, 30-32, 34, 85; and Normans, 30, 37; Venetians, 63

Agnes, daughter of Henry Jasomirgott, 105

Agnes, daughter of Louis VII, marriage to Alexius, 113, 120; marriage to Andronicus 122

Aix-la-Chapelle, treaty of, 14

Alexander III, Pope, 55, 86-87, 90-92, 96, 108, 110, 112-113, 117, 119-120, 137

Alexiad, 60, 131

Alexius I Comnenus, Byzantine emperor, 21, 27, 30, 34-38, 40, 42, 51, 53, 55, 147, 152

Alexius, presumptive heir of the Byzantine throne, 108; his marriage to Agnes Capet, 113, 120; coronation as co-emperor, 119

Alexius II, Byzantine emperor, 120-122

Alexius III, Byzantine emperor, 123

Alfonso of Aragon, 123

Almos, tribal chieftain of the Magyar people, 18

Almos, prince and governor of Croatia, 28-29, 100; and the em-

peror Henry IV, 30; conflict with King Coloman of Hungary, 34, 38-40, 93, 151; in Macedonian exile, 45; his death, 46-47

Amalfi, occupation by Roger II, 43

Amaury, king of Jerusalem, 117

Anacletus II, anti-Pope, 44

Anastasia, daughter of Yaroslav the Wise, 19

Ancona (city), envoys of Manuel at, 81; attacked by Barbarossa, 115; Byzantine ally, 117

Andrew I, king of Hungary, 19, 21, 46, 73; conflict with Byzantium, 20-21

Andronicus Comnenus, 80, 81, 83, 99, 103, 104, 120-122

Anna Comnena, daughter of Alexius I Comnenus, 38, 147

Annals of Ipat, 71

Anne of Châtillon, wife of Béla, king of Hungary, 109, 122

Antioch (city and principality), 34, 37, 49, 56, 60-61, 95

Apulia (duchy), 13, 16, 24, 43, 64, 81, 127; unification with Sicily, 44, 55, 58

Arabs: Byzantine campaign against, 17; Byzantine victory over (863), 12; in Southern Italy, 13; Venetian protection of Dalmatia against, 15

Arnold of Brescia, republican ruler of Rome, 76

Arnulf, king of Germany, 15, 17

Arpád, Hungarian leader, 18

Arpád dynasty, 18, 19, 25, 27, 29, 30, 32, 38, 53, 67, 87, 93, 149

Arpád princes, dispute with Salomon, 24

Augustinus, cardinal, papal legate, 33

Avlona (city), 72

Baldwin III, king of Jerusalem, 95

Balkans, 12, 61, 63, 71, 89, 95, 107, 124, 125; Byzantine-Bulgarian conflict for control, 15, 17; Byzantine military operations in, 43, 75, 83; Hungarian expansion in, 22, 32, 37, 47, 48, 50, 53; Manuel's policies and the, 56, 75, 79, 111, 112, 127, 128; Nicetas account on affairs in, 149; Norman Sicilian expansion in, 36, 37, 127; Robert Guiscard's plan to invade the, 36; Serbian revolt in, 64

Bánfi, Lucas, Hungarian archbishop of Esztergom, 86, 93, 96, 109, 110

Bari (city), 13, 16, 22, 52, 82

Basil I, Byzantine emperor, 12, 13, 14

Basil II, Byzantine emperor, 14-15, 20, 27

Beatrix of Burgundy, wife of Frederick I Barbarossa, 83

Béla I, prince, later king of Hungary, 19, 21, 149

Béla, prince, son of Almos, 45

Béla II, king of Hungary, 46-49, 52, 67, 69

Béla, Hungarian prince, brother of Stephen III, 97; appanage rights to Dalmatia and Sirmium, 100-103 107; engagement to Maria, Manuel's daughter and prospective heir to the Byzantine throne, 98, 99, 104, 108, 113, 119; marriage to Anne Châtillon, 109

Béla III, king of Hungary, 87, 109-110, 114, 115, 121-123, 128, 150

Béla IV, king of Hungary, 110

Belgrade (city), 22, 45, 73, 95, 122

Belos, prince, ban of Croatia and Dalmatia, guardian of King Géza II, 47-49, 67, 69-71, 74, 96, 153

Benevento, duke of, 13; duchy of, 16, 43

Berengar of Ivrea, usurper of the throne of Italy, 16

Bertha of Sulzbach, wife of Manuel I Comnenus, 44, 54, 60, 94

Biograd (Zaravecchia), 33

Bogislav, Michael, grand-zupan of Serbia, 27, 28, 51

Bodin, Constantine, zupan of Serbia, 27-28, 51, 52

Bohemond, prince of Antioch, son of Robert Guiscard, 34, 35, 37, 38, 42

Boleslav III, duke of Poland, 39

Bosnia (province), 27, 48, 49, 51, 52

Bosna (river), 48

Boris, illegitimate son of Coloman, pretender of Hungarian throne, 40, 47, 48, 62, 70, 74, 81, 84, 151-152

Branicevo (town in Serbia), 45, 46, 62, 74, 80, 122

Brindisi, siege of, 82

Bryennius, Byzantine commander, 82

Buda-Pest, capital of Hungary, 23

Bulgaria, Bulgars, 12, 15, 27, 51, 121, 123, 124

Burchard, imperial notary of Frederick I, 91

Busilla, Norman princess, wife of King Coloman, 32-34, 39, 41

Byzantine empire: alliances, 65; army, 106; control of Bari, 13; Bulgarian relations, 17; church, 20, 23; foreign policy, 12, 89, 91, 98, 125, 126; relations with Germany, 58-60, 64-66, 69, 71, 79, 90; relations with Hungary, 11, 23, 68, 74, 75, 77, 87, 97-99, 123, 147-148, 153; relations with Normans, 82, 89, 114, 115; relations with the papacy, 108, 113; Serbian conflict, 72, 73

Calabria (duchy), 13, 24, 43, 44, 55, 58, 64, 127

Cantacuzene, John, Byzantine commander of Belgrade, 80

Capua (city and duchy), 16, 44

Carpathians (mountain range), 11, 17

Cattaro (city in Dalmatia), 52, 71

Charlemagne, emperor of the Franks, 14, 16

Christian, archbishop of Mainz, 114, 119

Chronica Hungarorum, 151
Chronicle of Anonymus (*Gesta Hungarorum*), 150
Chronicon Budense, 150-151; *Pictum* (Marc de Kált), 150-151
Cilicia (province), 49, 56
Clement III, anti-pope, 29
Coloman, king of Hungary, 29-34, 41, 47, 50, 52, 56, 62, 70, 81, 93, 151; conflict with Almos, 38-40
Comnenian dynasty, 21, 30, 34, 53, 98, 119
Conrad I of Franconia, German king, 15
Conrad III, German emperor, 44, 48, 54, 55, 59-67, 69, 70, 72, 75-76, 78, 90, 101, 152
Conrad of Montferrat, capture of Archbishop Christian, 119
Constance, princess of Antioch, 49, 94, 109
Constance of Aragon, marriage to Emeric, 123
Constance of Hungary, daughter of Béla III, 123
Constance of Sicily, wife of emperor Henry VI, 121
Constance (city), treaty of (1153), 76-78
Constantine Bodin, *see* Bodin, 27-28, 51-52
Constantine VII Porphyrogenitus, Byzantine emperor, 25
Constantine VIII, Byzantine emperor, 20
Constantinople, 17, 36, 46, 52, 54, 56, 63, 64, 71-73, 148; as asylum of Hungarian pretenders, 40, 47, 74, 94; as capital of Roman empire, 55, 91, 92; government of, 45, 50
Corfu (island), 63, 64, 72, 116, 149
Council of Clermont (1095), 36; of Constantinople (1166), 100; of Pavia (1160), 90
Cresimir, Peter, prince of Croatia, 27
Croatia, 27-30, 32-34, 38, 49-50, 69, 100
Crown of St. Stephen, 25-26
Crusades: First, 30, 34, 36, 54, 60-61,

126, 147; failure of (1101), 37; Second, 52, 54, 56-57, 60-63, 65, 149, 151-152; Third, 121, 123; Fourth, 124, 126, 128, 148
Cumans (barbarian nomads), 22, 27-28, 63, 80, 106
Cyprus, conquest by Richard the Lionhearted, 121

Dalmatia (province), 13, 15, 27, 30-32, 34, 37-39, 41-43, 45, 49-50, 69, 100, 102-104, 107, 110-111, 116, 121
Dalmatian cities, 12, 14, 33, 123
Dalmatian coast, 27
Danube, 11, 16, 43, 73-75, 92, 112, 125, 153
De duabus civitatibus, 152
Denis, *comes palatinus* of Hungary, 94, 105-106
De profectione Ludovici VII in orientem, 151
Dessa (Stephen Nemanja), son of Uros of Rascia, 71, 79, 97
Diet of Regensburg (1152), 77, 152
Dioclea (Zeta), Byzantine vassal principality, 27-28, 44, 51, 71
Dniester (river), 11
Dolgoruki, George, prince of Suzdal, 68, 72
Drina (river), 48, 72
Dubrovnik (Ragusa), city in Dalmatia, 13
Ducas, John, Byzantine commander in So. Italy, 81-83, 104
Durazzo, *see* Dyrrhachium
Dyrrhachium (Durazzo), 35, 37

Edessa (city), 56, 60
Egypt, Byzantine attack on (853), 12
Eleanor of Aquitaine, 61
Emeric, Hungarian prince, son of Stephen I, 19
Emeric, Hungarian prince, son of Béla III, 123
Epirus, Norman attack on, 35
Euboea (island), Norman attack on, 63
Eugenius III, Pope, 53, 60, 65, 73, 75, 78

Euphemia, wife of Coloman, king of Hungary, 39, 47

Euphrates (river), expansion of Byzantine empire to, 56

Euphrosyne, Hungarian queen, wife of Géza II, 68, 93, 102, 109-110

Fischa (river), battle on the, 70, 71

France, attempted anti-Barbarossa alliance, 90; Bohemond's visit in, 37; Conrad III, 70; Hungarian expeditions against, 18; recognition of Pope Alexander III, 86

Francochorion, disputed territory between Byzantium and Hungary, 46, 73, 100, 111.

Frangepani, Roman family, 44

Franks, occupation of Venice by (809-810), 13; First Crusade, 36

Frederic I Barbarossa, German emperor, 55, 76, 78-79, 81-87, 90-94, 96, 101, 105, 110, 112, 113-115, 117-118, 120-121, 123, 152

Fulk, king of Jerusalem, 49

Gabras, Michael, Byzantine governor of Sirmium, 104, 106

Germany, Germans: emerging power in Central Europe, 15; relations with Byzantium, 16, 56, 61, 64, 66, 67, 69, 70, 71, 76, 77-79, 81, 83, 90, 92, 115; relations with Hungary, 18-19, 22, 28, 69, 70, 76, 77, 84-88, 105-106, 107; relations with Norman-Sicily, 115, 120; relations with the Papacy, 66, 76, 118; revolt against Conrad III, 64; treaty of Venice (1177) with Lombard communes, 118

Gesta Friderici I imperatoris, 152

Gesta Hungarorum, 150

Géza, Hungarian leader, 18

Géza I, king of Hungary, 20, 23-26, 28-30, 33

Géza II, king of Hungary, 48-49, 68-73, 75, 84-85, 87, 93-94, 96, 100-101, 152; Adriatic expansion, 85; relations with Byzantium, 74, 77, 79-81, 83, 87; relations with Norman-Sicily, 52, 79; relations with the

Papacy, 86, 87, 91; relations with Serbia (Rascia), 67, 68, 97; Second Crusade, 61-62

Gisella, Bavarian princess, marriage to Stephen I, 18

Godfrey of Bouillon, 30

Gregory VII, Pope, 24-26, 28, 29, 35, 36, 51

Guibertus (Clement III), anti-pope, 29

Guiscard, Robert, see Robert

Hadrian IV, Pope, 78, 81, 82, 86

Halich, principality, 67, 73, 107

Haram (town), 46

Helen, Hungarian queen, wife of Béla II, 47, 67

Helen (Ilona), wife of Zvonimir, king of Croatia, 28

Henry I, the Fowler, king of Germany, 15-16

Henry III, German emperor, 19, 23, 25, 77

Henry IV, German emperor, 21, 23-26, 28, 30, 39

Henry V, German emperor, 34

Henry, German prince, son of Conrad III, 48, 69

Henry VI, German prince, later emperor, son of Frederick I, 114, 115, 119, 121

Henry of Babenberg (Jasomirgott), duke of Austria, 70, 71, 77, 96, 105, 107, 110, 152

Henry the Lion, duke of Bavaria, 77

Henry the Proud, duke of Bavaria, 65

Hohenstaufen dynasty, 44, 126, 127; empire, 112, 119

Honorius II, Pope, 43-44

"Hun-Chronicle" (Simeon of Kézai), 150

Hungary, Hungarians: army tactics, 106; conflict with Bulgarians, 17; conversion to Christianity, 18; first appearance in Europe, 11-12, 17, 145; passage of Crusaders, 30, 61-62; Pecheneg invasion of, 21; rapprochement with Venice, 104; relations with Byzantium, 17, 18-23, 56-57, 66-67, 70, 73-75, 81, 83-84, 87,

93-94, 97, 99, 102, 104-108, 110-112, 114-116, 125, 127-28; relations with France, 110, 123; relations with Germany, 15, 18-19, 76-77, 84-86, 93, 105, 114; relations with Kiev, 71, 72; relations with Normans, 30, 33; relations with Papacy, 25, 85-87; relations with Serbians, 66-68, 71-72, 127; Slavic cooperation, 47, 51, 68, 79, 107; throne succession, 85, 93, 94, 95, 117, 149

Iconium, sultan of, 57, 60
Ilona (Helen) *see* Helen
Innocent II, Pope, 44
Irene, empress, wife of John II Comnenus, 38, 40, 54
Isaac Angelus, Byzantine emperor, 121-123, 148
Isaac Comnenus, Byzantine emperor, 21
Isaac Comnenus, (Sebastocrator), brother of John II, 80, 85
Isiaslav, prince of Pereyaslavl, 68, 71-72
Italy: Byzantine-German cooperation in, 61, 64-65; Byzantine intervention in, 64, 72, 75, 79, 81-84, 89; Byzantine possessions in, 12-13, 21, 34-36; German intervention in, 16, 75-76, 78-79, 81-82, 127; Manuel's policies in, 53, 55-57, 59, 63, 92, 98, 112-113, 115, 120, 125, 127-128; Norman expansion in southern, 44, 61

Jacquinta, widow of Constantine Bodin, 52
Jerusalem, king of, 49, 60
John, commander of Byzantine forces in support of Béla III, 109
John II, Comnenus, Byzantine emperor, 30, 38, 40, 42-47, 49-55, 58, 59, 67, 69, 147-148, 152
John Comnenus, nephew of Manuel, 80
John Roger, *caesar,* son-in-law of John II Comnenus, 54, 59
John XII, Pope, 16
John of Salisbury, 90

Judith, daughter of Henry III, wife of Salomon, King of Hungary, 19

Karas (river), 46
Kiev (city and principality), 68, 71, 73, 93
Kilidj Arslan, sultan of Iconium, 57, 58, 94, 110, 115, 117, 118, 127
Kontostephanos, Alexius, commander of Byzantine army, 97
Kontostephanos, Andronicus, Manuel's nephew, commander of Byzantine army, 105, 107

Ladislas, son of Béla I, rivalry with Salomon, 23
Ladislas I, king of Hungary, 26-30, 32, 33, 38, 39, 50, 53, 100
Ladislas, son of Coloman, 33
Ladislas, son of Béla II, prince of Bosnia, 49, 87, 94, 95
Ladislas II, king of Hungary, 95, 96
Lascaris, Theodore, Byzantine emperor, 148
Latin princes and Manuel, 56, 61
Latins, contact with Greeks during Crusades, 36, 54
Lay investiture, 24, 25, 26, 28-30, 33, 133
Lechfeld, Hungarian defeat at (955), 18
Legnano, victory of Lombard League at (1176), 117
Leo III, Byzantine emperor, 11
Leo V, Byzantine emperor, 12
Leo VI, Byzantine emperor, 17
Leo IX, Pope, 19
Liudprand, bishop of Cremona, 16
Lombard army, 52; cities, 24, 86, 112, 117, 118; Lombard League, 108, 117, 140
Lombards, Byzantine loss of Ravenna to, 12
Lothair I, Frankish emperor, alliance with Venice, 13-14
Lothair II,. German emperor, 44, 55
Lothair, king of Italy, 16
Louis II, emperor and king of Italy, son of Lothair I, 13
Louis the Child, king of Germany, 15

Louis VII, king of France, 53, 60-63, 74, 86, 87, 91, 113, 119-120, 151-152

Lucas, Archbishop, see Bánfi, Lucas, archbishop

Luitpold, Markgraf of Austria, 42

Macedonia (province), 17, 40, 43, 45-46

Macedonian dynasty, 12, 20

Magyars, see also Hungarians, 11, 17-18

Manuel I, Comnenus, Byzantine emperor, 38, 53, 54, 60, 63, 71, 79, 80, 94, 98, 103, 109, 113, 119-120, 122, 136, 148-149, 152; campaigns against Iconium, see also Kilidj Arslan, 57, 117, 118; and crusaders, 62, 63; foreign policy of, 42, 55-56, 58-59, 75, 82, 89, 91, 92, 98, 107-108, 112-113, 115, 117-118, 125-127; relations with Germany, 44, 64, 67, 76-79, 81-82, 84, 87, 89-90, 105; relations with Hungary, 47, 50, 66, 73-75, 83-85, 87-88, 91, 93-110, 121, 125-128, 141; relations with Kiev, 68; relations with Lombard League, 108, 118; relations with Norman-Sicily, 61, 64, 66, 72, 75, 77, 81, 83, 89, 91-92, 114-115, 117; relations with Papacy, 76, 91-92, 112; relations with Serbia, 65, 72, 79, 111; relations with Venice, 116

Manzikert, battle of (1071), 21-22

Marc of Kált, Hungarian medieval historian, 150-151

Margaret Capet, wife of Béla III, 123

Margaret, daughter of Béla III, wife of Isaac Angelus, 122

Margaret, Norman-Sicilian queen, widow of William I, 113

Maria, Byzantine princess, daughter of John II, 54, 59

Maria, Byzantine princess, daughter of Manuel, 97-99, 108-109, 113-114, 115, 119, 122, 143-145

Maria, Byzantine princess, cousin of Manuel, 78, 85, 94

Marie of Antioch, Byzantine empress, wife of Manuel, 94, 108-109, 121-122, 145

Maritza (river), 45

Mas'ud, Sultan of Iconium, 57

Melfi, treaty of (1059), 24

Michael I, Byzantine emperor, 14

Michael III, Byzantine emperor, 12

Michael VII, Ducas, Byzantine emperor, 22-23, 25-28, 35-36, 51

Michieli, Domenico, doge of Venice, 42

Milan (city), 108, 112

Mogyorod, battle of, 23

Montenegro (Zeta, province), 27, 51

Montpellier (city), 90

Morava (river), 45, 48, 72-73, 122

Moravian kingdom, 15, 17

Mstislav, grand prince of Kiev, 68, 102

Myriocephalon, defeat of Byzantine army at (1176), 58, 117-118, 128

Naissus, see Nis.

Nemanja, Stephen (Dessa), Serbian zupan, 71, 79, 97, 111, 122, 141

Nera (river), 46

Nicephorus I, Byzantine emperor, 14

Nicephorus II, Phocas, Byzantine emperor, 16

Nicephorus III, Botaniates, Byzantine emperor, 23, 36

Nicephorus, Bryennius, husband of Anna Comnena, 147

Nicholas II, Pope, 23-24

Nis (Naissus, city), 22, 45, 80, 97, 122

Norman, Normans: aid to papacy, 24; alliance with Louis VII, 61; alliance with Venice, 117; appearance in Europe, 11; Barbarossa's policy against, 76; Byzantine-German alliance against, 56-60; conflicts with Byzantium under Alexius I, 35-37; cooperation with Hungary, 30, 32-34, 52, 79; loss of Southern Italy to, 21-22; loss of Thessalonica under Andronicus to, 122; Manuel's campaigns against, 63-64, 66, 72, 75, 78, 82-83, 89, 116, 127, 149; mercenaries in Byzantine army, 106;

peaceful relations with Byzantium, 59; threat to Byzantine empire, 42-44, 58, 61
Norman-Sicily, alliance with Byzantium against Germany, 90-92; and Barbarossa, 76; Byzantine-German alliance against, 60; expansion in Southern Italy, 61, 127; relations with Byzantium, 81, 89-90, 94, 112-114, 128; relations with Hungary, 52, 56, 79; *see* also Norman, Normans
Nur-ed-din, atabeg of Mosul, 117, 127

Ochrida, Byzantine occupation of, 20
Odo of Deuil (historian), 151
Oguz (nomadic people), attacks on Pechenegs, 22
Onogurs, 11
Orseolo, Peter, doge of Venice, 15
Orseolo, Otto, doge of Venice, 19
Otto, duke of Moravia, 23
Otto I, the Great, German emperor, 16, 18
Otto II, German emperor, 16
Otto of Freising (historian), 40, 47, 77, 151-152
Otto of Wittelsbach, 105

Paleologus, Michael, Byzantine commander in Italian campaign of Manuel, 81-83
Paleologus, George, Manuel's envoy to Hungary, 97
Palermo (city), 59, 63, 66
Palestine, 56, 61, 126
Papacy, breach with Roger II, 65; claim for supreme authority, 90; conflict with Hungary, 25; independence from secular power, 23-24; power factor in Italy, 112
Pantokrator, monastery of, 38
Particiacus, Ursus, doge of Venice, 13
Patzinaks, *see* Pechenegs
Pavia, council of, 86
Pechenegs (nomadic people), in Black Sea area, 11; conflict with Hungarians, 17, 21-22; invasion of

Thrace and Macedonia, 43; participation in Serbian revolt, 72; troops in Byzantine army, 106
Pécsvárad, monastery of, 40
Peloponnesus, Norman invasion of, 63, 149
"Peoples Crusade," 30
Pervoslav, zupan of Rascia, 49, 71-72, 79, 97
Peter, king of Hungary, 19
Philip of Alsace, count of Flanders, intermediary between Manuel and Louis VII, 119-120
Philip Augustus, king of France, 123
Philippopolis, city in Thrace, 45-46, 63, 95
Pierleoni, Roman family, 44
Piroska (Irene), Hungarian princess, marriage to John Comnenus, 38
Pascal II, Pope, 33
Pozsony, city in Hungary, 23, 26, 70, 95
Predslava, Kievan princess, wife of Almos, 39
Prizren (city), Constantin Bodin's coronation, 27
Przemysl, "royal road" through, 68

Radoslav, zupan of Zeta, 71
Ragusa, city in Dalmatia, 13, 27; Hungarian conquest of, 33; Venetian attack on, 116
Rama, province, *see* Bosnia
Rascia, vassal principality of Byzantium, 27, 44, 47, 49; alliance with Hungary, 48, 50-52; Serbian independence movement, 43, 51
Ratislav, prince of Kiev, treaty with Byzantium, 102
Ravenna, city lost by Byzantium, 12
Raymond of Poitiers, prince of Antioch, 61, 94; conflict with John II Comnenus, 49; homage to Byzantium, 56
Regensburg (city), meeting of Hungarian envoys and crusaders, 62; Barbarossa's arbitration in Hungarian throne dispute, 94
Renier of Montferrat, husband of

Maria, Manuel's daughter, 119, 122, 145

Richard the Lionhearted, king of England, conquest of Cyprus, 121

Robert, Count of Capua, conspiracy against Manuel, 59

Robert, Count of Loritello, Norman rebel leader against William I, 81

Robert, Guiscard, duke of Apulia, 22, 30, 32, 34-35, 43; plans to invade Byzantium, 36; relations with Papacy, 24, 33

Roger I, count of Sicily, 32, 43

Roger, duke of Apulia, son of Robert Guiscard, 35

Roger II, king of Sicily, 58-59, 65, 81, 121; conflict with Pope Eugenius III, 65, 75; Hungarian-Norman cooperation, 52, 79; Manuel's policies against, 64, 75, 78, 149; role in Serbian revolt, 64-65, 71; Second Crusade, 61, 63; unification of Sicily and Southern Italy, 43-44, 55, 58, 127

Romanus IV, Byzantine emperor, 118

Rudolf, duke of Swabia, elected king of Germany, 26

St. Bernard of Clairvaux, 60

Saladin, Moslem leader, Sultan of Egypt and Syria, 127

Salerno (city and duchy), Byzantine vassalage, 13, 43

Salomon, king of Hungary, engagement to Judith, daughter of Henry III, 19; relations with Henry IV, 21; attack on Byzantium, 22; rivalry with cousins Géza and Ladislas, 23, 26; relations with Gregory VII, 24; in possession of St. Stephen's crown, 25; in exile, 27

Samuel, tsar of Bulgaria, struggle with Basil II, 20

Saracens, threat to Western Europe, 11; loss of Sicily to, 12; attacks on Byzantine possessions, 12-14; reconquest of Bari from, 13

Sardica (Sophia, city), Hungarian troops in, 122

Sava (river), 46, 73, 106

Seljuk Turks, attacking Byzantine empire, 21-22, 35

Semlin (Zemun), fortress, 46; surrender of, 73, 103; battle with Hungarians near, 105-106

Serbia, Byzantine interest in, 57; cooperation with Hungary, 50-52; independence movement, 48, 53, 124

Serbians: see also Serbia; Hungarian support to, 43, 50, 98; Manuel's campaigns against, 56; revolt against Byzantium, 51, 64-66, 71-72, 79, 111, 121, 127, 149

Sicily, see also Norman Sicily; crusaders, 61; loss to Saracens, 12; Manuel's policies toward, 59, 66, 71, 89, 108, 112-113, 115; relations with Papacy, 82, 86; unification with Apulia and Calabria, 43-44, 55, 58

Simeon, Bulgarian tsar, invasion of Macedonia and Thrace, 17

Simeon of Kézai, author of Gesta Hungarorum, 150-151

Sirmium (city), in Hungarian possession, 21, 46, 102-103, 121; Byzantine attack on, 73; in Byzantine possession, 104, 107, 110-111

Skadar (Scutari), town in Zeta, Byzantine occupation of, 52

Slavs, Byzantine influence, 12; raids on Dalmatia, 14-15; raids on Germany, 15

Sobieslav II, duke of Bohemia, relations with Béla III, 110

Sophia, Hungarian princess, daughter of Béla II, 48, 69

Sophia (Sardica, city), see also Sardica, 45, 95, 122

Spain, Conrad III's interests, 70; recognition of Pope Alexander III, 86

Spalato (Split, city), in Byzantine possession, 13; coronation of Zvonimir at, 28; Hungarian conquest of, 33

Split, see Spalato

Stephen I, king of Hungary, 18-19, 20, 25-26; Hungary after conversion of, 149; canonization of, 27

Stephen II, king of Hungary, 33, 40-

41, 67; campaigns of, 41-42, 45-46; conspiracy of Boris against, 47
Stephen III, king of Hungary, son of Géza II, 84, 87, 93, 109, 114, 117, 151; relations with Henry Jasomirgott, 105, 107; relations with Mannuel, 94, 96-98, 100-103, 107, 116, 149; support from Barbarossa, 96
Stephen IV, king of Hungary, brother of Géza II, relations with Byzantium, 80, 94-95, 97, 99, 103; throne disputes with Stephen III, 84-85, 87; opposition in Hungary against, 96, 100, 102
Suger, French minister, anti-Byzantine attitude, 65
Svatopluk, king of Moravia, 15, 17
Svyatopolk, son of Vladislav, king of Bohemia, 101
Svyatopolk II, grand prince of Kiev, 39
Sylvester II, Pope, 19, 25-26
Synnadena, wife of Géza I, king of Hungary, 23
Syria (province), 21, 49, 56, 60-61, 126

Tancred, prince of Antioch, nephew of Bohemond, 37
Temes (river), Boris' invasion in valley of, 73
Thebes (Greek city), Norman occupation of, 63
Theodora, Byzantine empress, daughter of Constantine VIII, 20
Theodora, Byzantine princess, niece of Manuel Comnenus, 54; marriage with Henry of Babenberg, 71, 77
Theodora, Byzantine princess, sister of Manuel Comnenus, 122
Theophano, Byzantine princess, wife of emperor Otto II, 16
Theophilus, Byzantine emperor, 12
Thessalonica (city), 17; visit of Conrad III, 64; conquest by Normans, 121-122
Thessaly (province), Alexius' defensive war against Normans, 35
Thrace (province), Bulgarian invasion of, 17; Hungarians defeated in, 19; Pecheneg invasion of, 43
Thuroczy, Joannes (historian), 151
Titel (town), Manuel's headquarters at, 101
Transylvania (province), Byzantine invasion of, 104; German settlers in, 69
Traù (city), 13; Hungarian conquest of, 33; Venetian attack on, 116
Trogir, *see* Traù
Turks, *see* also Seljuk Turks, 34, 56-58; auxiliaries in Byzantine army, 106; campaigns against, 49, 110, 118
Tzimisces, John, Byzantine emperor, 16

Urban II, Pope, 28-29, 36
Uros, zupan of Rascia, 47-48, 52, 71

Valona (Avlona, city), 72
Vatatzes, Theodore, Byzantine commander of the siege of Semlin, 73
Venetian, Venetians, *see* also Venice; alliance with Lothair I, 14; attacks on Dalmatia, 41, 143; trade monopolies in Byzantium, 15, 35, 42, 63, 116
Venice (republic), aid to Byzantium, 35, 63-64, 103; alliance with Norman-Sicily, 116-117; conflicts with Hungary, 85, 121; conflict with Manuel, 107-108, 112-113, 116, 128; defense of Dalmatia, 15, 32-34; independence of, 12-14; rapprochment with Hungary, 104; treaty of (1177), 117-118
Victor III, Pope, 36
Victor IV, anti-Pope, 86, 90-91
Visegrad, royal castle in Hungary, Salomon imprisoned in, 26
Vladimir II, Monomach, grand prince of Kiev, 39, 68
Vladimirko, prince of Halich, 68, 72-73, 101
Vladislav, king of Bohemia, 84; aid to Stephen III, 96, 101; friendship with Manuel, 101, 103

Welf, duke of Bavaria, revolt against Conrad III, 65

Wibald, abbot of Corvey, 78

William I, king of Sicily, 66, 81; conflict with Byzantium, 82; peace treaty with Manuel, 89, 91-92

William II, king of Sicily, proposed marriage to Maria, Manuel's daughter, 113, 115, 119; negotiations with Frederick, 115; alliance with Venice, 116; conquest of Thessalonica, 121

William, prince of Apulia, Robert Guiscard's grandson, 43

William, marquis of Montferrat, 119

William of Pavia, cardinal, papal legate to Manuel's court, 91

Xeros, Basil, Byzantine ambassador to Roger II, 59

Yaroslav, prince of Halich, 101, 103, 105

Yaroslav the Wise, prince of Kiev, 19

Zadar, see Zara

Zara, (Zadar) city in Dalmatia, 13, 27, 33; Hungarian occupation of, 34, 85, 121; in Venetian possession, 41

Zaravecchia (Biograd, city), 33; destroyed by Venetians, 41

Zemun, see Semlin

Zeta (Dioclea), vassal principality of Byzantium, 27, 44, 51, 71

Ziani, Sebastiano, doge of Venice, negotiations with Manuel, 116

Zoe, Byzantine empress, daughter of Constantine VIII, 20

Zvonimir, king of Croatia, 28, 32

GERMAN EMPIRE

POLAND

DANUBE

Regensburg

A U S T R I A

Vienna

Pozsony (Pressburg)

TISZA

Esztergom

Buda·Pest

H U N G A R Y

DRAVA

Milan

Republic of Venice

C R O A T I A

SAVA

Petrikon

T R A N S Y L V A N

PO

Genoa

PAPAL STATE

B O S N I A

Sirmium

Semlin

Belgrade

Branicevo

P E C I

Pisa

Florence

D A L M A T I A

Zara

Trau

Spalato

R A S C I A

Z E T A

MORAVA

Nis

DA

Ancona

Sardica (Sofia)

A D R I A T I C   S E A

Ragusa

Cattaro

Rome

Benevento

Bari

Dyrrhachium

Thessalonica

Naples

A P U L I A

Brindisi

Avlona

T Y R R H E N I A N   S E A

Taranto

CALABRIA

I O N I A N   S E A

CORFU

A E G

EUBOEA

N O R M A N   S I C I L Y

Athens

Palermo

SICILY

Corinth

P E L O P O N N E S U S

CR

M E D I T E R R A N E A N   S E A